THE DRINKING CURRICULUM

The Drinking Curriculum

A CULTURAL HISTORY OF CHILDHOOD AND ALCOHOL

Elizabeth A. Marshall

FORDHAM UNIVERSITY PRESS   NEW YORK   2024

A grant from Simon Fraser University's publication fund contributed to the costs associated with producing this book.

Visit us online at www.fordhampress.com.

Library of Congress Cataloging-in-Publication Data available online at https://catalog.loc.gov.

Printed in the United States of America

26 25 24   5 4 3 2 1

First edition

Contents

THE DRINKING CURRICULUM

Introduction

Learning to Drink

In *The Little Boy and His Mother* published in 1833, a young boy reaches eagerly for a glass of rum sweetened with sugar (see Figure 1).[1] A dialogue between a fictional child reader and his mother ensues.

> CHILD: Will he be a drunkard, mother?
>
> MOTHER: I cannot tell; but I should think he is in a fair way to that end. He has the appetite of a drunkard, in the same proportion as he has the size of a man.
>
> CHILD: Will his mother give him some rum and sugar, does mother think?
>
> MOTHER: Very likely; for a great many parents thoughtlessly include their children in their foolish and injurious demands, in addition to setting them a bad example.

Alcohol is frequently pictured in U.S. culture in advertisements, TV shows, cartoons, film, and comics as well as in children's books like *The Little Boy and His Mother*. Perhaps most surprising for twenty-first-century readers, children drink.

Indeed, a curriculum about the pleasures and pitfalls of alcohol has been in place in visual culture for almost two centuries. Often assumed to be the soberest of spaces, texts for or about the child are anything but. The example that opens this book might seem like an anachronism. Surely drinking children are a thing of the past, and adults in the twenty-first century know better than to visualize underage imbibing in a book for children, even if it is a cautionary tale. Yet, drinking and drunk children hide in plain sight.

Figure 1. Illustration from *The Little Boy and His Mother* (1833). Courtesy, American Antiquarian Society.

This is a curious claim to make because for decades adults have concerned themselves with the appropriateness of what children read and view, attempting to police childhood's borders into a G-rated haven. For instance, one common approach for studying alcohol in children's texts, advertisements, and other media typically employed in education, communication, health, and psychology focuses on the potential dangers of its appearance in visual and material culture.[2] Countless studies document the potential risks to actual children who consume fictional portrayals of drinking and drunkenness. The logic goes something like this: If youth are exposed to the wine-toting Little Red Riding Hood in Trina Schart Hyman's 1983 picture book (challenged in the 1990s for "promoting alcohol to youth"), popping champagne bottles in Disney's *Beauty and the Beast*, pro-alcohol messages on T-shirts from Urban Outfitters, or as one *New York Times* reporter put it, the "jarring" images of teen drinking in the 2009 film *Harry Potter and the Half-Blood Prince*, then they will be more susceptible to substance abuse.[3] Research on the frequency of and exposure to representations of drinking in children's media is no doubt an important line of inquiry. However, as James Kincaid notes, stories of protection are "also stories of incitement; the denials are always affirmations."[4] The image of the rum-loving boy, for example, both disavows and confirms alcohol's gratifications. Simply put, while mainstream culture invests a lot of energy pearl-clutching about the child's exposure to harm, the texts created for and consumed by children repeatedly tempt them into the delights of intoxication.

This book investigates that paradox by bringing to light what I call "the drinking curriculum," a set of cultural lessons that rely on images of fictionalized childhood to animate adult anxieties and preoccupations about alcohol. This is a cradle-to-grave program that teaches through visual culture and that relies on both horror and humor to educate. The drinking curriculum doesn't follow a linear progression and there are no lock-step stages of development to be assessed. Alcohol's presence is at once omnipresent and indiscernible, and to understand this "requires a mixture of seeing and learning not to see."[5] One of the drinking curriculum's most enduring outcomes is that it teaches us how not to see alcohol, even as images of drinking, drunkenness, and childhood consistently flicker in the background.

To that end, the following pages examine "the child" and alcohol in popular visual texts. The child in this study is a functional figure, "a malleable part of our discourse rather than a fixed stage; 'the child' is a product of ways of perceiving, not something that is *there*."[6] Thus, this book is not about how real children might respond to or be influenced by texts about intoxication, but rather how the categories of childhood and alcohol shape one another. This is not to deny the dangers associated with underage drinking, which the Centers for Disease Control and Prevention defines as "a significant public health problem in the U.S," or the material conditions in which youth are put in harm's way.[7] Nor is this book about the potential risks to witnessing images of alcoholism for children who live with alcoholics. Rather, it is concerned with how the idea of the child and its associations with innocence, vulnerability, wildness, and misbehavior all inhere within our perceptions of sobriety and intoxication.

Of course, the child is a worthy and admirable focus of concern, and no one would question advocating for children's welfare. But the volatility of alcohol in the drinking curriculum's imagery combines with complex and even contradictory adult feelings that get projected onto children—they are precious, they are unpredictable, they act in ways adults can't get away with and are jealous of, even as adults control children. In this way, adult anxieties about a whole host of issues—immigration, sex, violence, mental and physical vulnerability—are projected onto the figure of the child and animated by alcohol. The drinking curriculum answers questions about childhood and drinking by putting the adult back in the frame. The restoration of this figure to the scene of instruction reveals that adults themselves are also the subjects of these ongoing lessons.

The questions addressed in the pages that follow include: Why do we need the child to teach us about alcohol? Why is the alignment of alcohol, drunkenness, and childhood so scandalous? When and to what ends do the child and alcohol appear in visual culture? Who "profits" from the circulation of these familiar images of intoxication and "who pays the price?"[8] *The Drinking*

Curriculum answers these questions as it moves across visual culture, social histories of drinking, and childhood studies.

Childhood, Alcohol, and Innocence

An ongoing reckoning with and public sentiment about alcohol consumption swings wildly across the history of the United States. In the 1820s rum was cheaper to buy in New England than tea; in 1919 the passing of the Volstead Act made the manufacture and sale of alcoholic beverages illegal.[9] Cocktail culture flowered in the 1950s, as did the drinking habits of teenagers, while in the twenty-first century neo-temperance trends like #sobercurious or mindful drinking flourish, illustrating how culture and alcohol interact. These examples reveal more than the mere cycling of attitudes toward alcohol, or the corrective swinging of a pendulum from enthusiasm to restraint; rather, they demonstrate ongoing contestations about drinking and drunkenness.

The history of alcohol in the United States focuses almost exclusively on adults who advocated temperance, brewed beer, created speakeasies, campaigned for or against alcohol, and passed legislation that prohibited drinking. Histories from Andrew Barr's *Drink: A Social History of America* to Susan Cheever's *Drinking in America: Our Secret History* and Daniel Okrent's *Last Call: The Rise and Fall of Prohibition*, include children as footnotes within a larger adult drama.[10] Yet, youth were and continue to be used as symbols in national education campaigns whether in the temperance movement or in the charge to create a national minimum drinking age in the 1980s, illustrating the broader culture's vexed relationship with alcohol. While not always the main figure in scenes of intoxication, the child makes a regular appearance. Importantly, pictures of children, whether sober, drinking, or drunk "are a form of ideas, not reality."[11] The child in the viewer's line of sight might be obstructed or spotlighted to amplify or downplay agency, vulnerability, and even depravity.

Thus, childhood in the drinking curriculum is elastic, snapping into place in different time periods and for different causes. In the current moment, chronological age defines when, where, and who can consume alcohol. Yet, this is a recent invention. Before Prohibition, parents controlled if children drank, and after the repeal of the eighteenth amendment, states passed drinking age laws.[12] It is not until passage of the 1984 National Minimum Drinking Age Act that all states adopted 21 as the legal age to purchase or publicly consume alcohol. Even as access to alcohol marks the legal end of childhood, categories of age are always under construction.[13] In this book, the term childhood is often used as a shorthand for both the child and the adolescent because categories of age are themselves unsteady. Even more to the point, it is the contention of this book that drunkenness blurs any fixed line between adulthood and childhood.

Blog posts like "20 Ways your Toddler is Just Like Your Drunk Friend" on *Scary Mommy* or videos on YouTube such as "Drunk vs. Kid" define shared traits of emotional outbursts, required supervision, and loss of bodily comportment, underscoring seemingly common-sense associations between drunk adults and young children.[14] Thus, "childish deviance bears a striking resemblance to the behavior of adults when faced with drunkenness, which itself often manifests as childishness."[15] Of course, these ideas have a history. The connection between childishness and drunkenness was in place in the cultural imagination by at least the mid-nineteenth century (see Figure 2). C.S. Reinhart's 1874 sketch for *Harper's Weekly*, "The Poor Drunkard—More Helpless than a Child" evinces this connection, picturing an intoxicated man unable to stand on his own and whose lack of physical and intellectual ability marks his child-like immaturity.

Youth in the sketch are pedagogical objects in a visual argument about failed white manhood. The father turns away from his wife and son in the right foreground toward the white middle-class children on the left side of the image who stand steadfastly staring at the fallen man, their innocence, futurity, and

Figure 2. Charles Stanley Reinhart's 1874 "The Poor Drunkard—More Helpless Than a Child," *Harper's*. Courtesy, American Antiquarian Society.

moral superiority signified by the white light shining from the top left of the image. The drunkard in Reinhart's illustration leans to his right into the darker shaded side of the image, dangling his pocket watch in exchange for money for drink, intemperate and ill-behaved. Reinhart's portrayal of children employed them as markers of goodness and sobriety. However, this was only one representation.

Tipsy Tots and Where to Find Them

Images of children have been used both to teach about the harm of alcohol consumption and to market its pleasures. In nineteenth-century temperance texts, children are disposable, often quickly eradicated by a drunk adult or by liquor itself. In *The Glass of Whisky* (1860) published by the American Sunday School Union, a 6-year-old boy inadvertently drinks a jug of rum from a closet and dies in the street (see Figure 3). Temperance advocates used cautionary tales like this one to emphasize that even a sip of alcohol would lead

Figure 3. Illustration from *The Glass of Whisky* (1860). Courtesy, American Antiquarian Society.

to harm, including death. The text expands the visual message: "He tasted it. He liked it. He tasted a little more. Then he drank a good deal. At last he became drunk, fell over, and lay there till he died. He was found dead by the jug of rum."[16] Like the bottle, the dead white boy is symbolic, a fictional casualty in the nineteenth-century culture war waged around alcohol.

Relatedly, pictures of immigrant children drinking alcohol sought to make an argument about the corrupting influence of outsiders. In "Sketches of the People who Oppose our Sunday Laws," a schoolgirl in pigtails and a baby drink from steins in a German beer garden. The young girl eagerly downs the last drop of her mug of beer. On the balcony a sign instructs revelers "not to stand on the chairs or tables" and a woman tries to convince an intoxicated man to step down from a table; behind her, a pickpocket waits to strike (see Figure 4). Here, the drinking child symbolizes the corruption of German immigrants who in temperance discourse "were perceived as boisterous, immoral, nonproductive, and ultimately detrimental to the Republic."[17]

The sketch reflects a debate about liquor laws, like those put in place by the New York State Assembly in 1857 that "reduced the number of saloon

A GERMAN BEER GARDEN IN NEW YORK CITY ON SUNDAY EVENING.

Figure 4. "A German Beer Garden in New York City on Sunday Evening" (1857) *Harper's*. Courtesy, American Antiquarian Society

licenses available in the city, placed limits on the amount an individual was allowed to drink and ordered all liquor-dealing establishments to close on Sundays" as a way "to force New York's ethnic underclasses to observe the sabbath in what was deemed an appropriate manner."[18] The nativist sentiments of the temperance movement are communicated through the drinking child, a sign of the community's immorality. Alcohol and immigrants were both damaging influences and a threat to the social fabric of the United States. The *Harper's* political cartoon also confirms varying cultural, religious, and ethnic conventions about childhood drinking. While temperance advocates regularly manipulated images of children in their efforts to ban alcohol, youngsters were also front and center in the marketing of alcoholic beverages.

Throughout the late nineteenth and early twentieth centuries, corporations like Pabst Brewing Company and Rainier Beer used drinking children in advertising campaigns to advocate for the health benefits of alcohol (see Figure 5). A 1906 advertisement for the Seattle Brewing and Malting Company promotes school-age drinking, once an accepted idea that now seems unimaginable. A girl holds a beer in hand toasting "Gesundheit Grandpa." Grandfather and granddaughter look at one another, eyes locked, toasting from two equal-sized frothy glasses. The girl celebrates her youth and grandpa the glow of his second childhood. The young girl's presence makes positive associations between alcohol consumption via youth's vitality and futurity. The Seattle Brewing and Malting Company and other beverage companies teach about alcohol and intoxication through a pedagogy of pleasure that, like fear, is a signature of the drinking curriculum. These are just a small sampling of tipsy tots in visual culture, but they give us a starting point to consider how the drinking curriculum gives expression to a culture preoccupied with competing impulses toward alcohol in relation to childhood: temperance and intemperance, sanctimony and debauchery, fear and laughter.

Horror and Humor

To be sure, alcoholism is no laughing matter, and as periodic public awareness campaigns and health and safety statistics make clear, alcohol and suffering are causes for concern. However, if the drinking curriculum is the vehicle that delivers lessons about alcohol, humor is riding in the sidecar. Fear and pleasure, violence and comedy coexist in representations of intoxication from the little boy who loved rum in the nineteenth century to the hard-partying baby in Johannes Nyholm's 2011 award-winning film, *Las Palmas*.[19] Philoso-

Figure 5. 1906 advertisement for Rainier Beer. Courtesy, University of Washington Libraries, Special Collections, ADV0304.

pher Noël Carroll writes that an intimate relationship exists between horror and humor, which are two sides of the same coin, linked "to the problematization, violation, and transgression of standing categories, norms, and concepts."[20] Through intoxication, the category of childhood as a state of innocence is consistently violated via fear or pleasure. Whether cautionary or humorous, alcohol and the discourses around it express a deeply entrenched cultural ambivalence about children.

Writing in 1979 for *Time* magazine, one cultural critic defined this ambivalence as "a pervasive, low-grade child-aversion in the U.S."[21] Misopedic impulses have long been communicated within texts created for and consumed by children, snaking through childhood's library from fairy tales to film.[22] So, too, in his study of "The Dead Baby Joke Cycle" Alan Dundes argues there is a sick streak "and a longstanding one at that—in American humor" that is anti-child.[23] In the drinking curriculum, drunkenness provides a culturally sanctioned outlet for picturing violence and humor, expressing how "all kinds of aversions to and adorations of children occur simultaneously."[24] Throughout this book, readers will confront drinking humor packaged as comedic violence that takes aim at children, childlike Others, and childish objects.

In Edward Gorey's subversive and satirical alphabet book *The Gashlycrumb Tinies: or, After the Outing* (1963), for example, Z stands for Zillah who drank too much gin (see Figure 6). Zillah's demise parodies cautionary temperance narratives in which children die from the overconsumption of alcohol in titles like *The Glass of Whisky* (see Figure 3). Gorey's visual humor, like slapstick, "never lingers on the violence, in fact, he invests it with no emotion at all" which tilts his work toward the comic.[25] Further exemplifying child harm as a form of humor, when asked in an interview about why his numerous victims are often children Gorey replied, "It's just so obvious. They're the easiest targets."[26] The suffering child is a manifestation of the "complex relationship between vulnerability and violence" and the object of both sympathy and mirth.[27]

Studies of humor suggest that laughter can be a response to violence, and comedy like the death of Zillah can be "dark, twisted stuff."[28] Laughter releases the tension "between the pleasure the joke gives us and our simultaneous feeling that we shouldn't laugh in the circumstances. Dark humor hits the funny bone in two ways."[29] Not all humor is amusing and not everyone will laugh at the same things. Ultimately, however, whether one finds drunk children funny or not is beside the point. Drinking child humor is a hallmark of the drinking curriculum, and it is here to stay. Matt Groening's

Z is for ZILLAH who drank too much gin

Figure 6. "Z is for Zillah," Edward Gorey, *The Gashlycrumb Tinies, or After the Outing* (1963). Image used with permission from The Edward Gorey Charitable Trust.

The Simpsons provides an example. In "Homer vs. the Eighteenth Amendment" Springfield hosts a Saint Patrick's Day parade.[30] Duff beer flows with so much gusto that the beverage inadvertently fills Bart's toy horn, after which he burps and teeters and his eyes go to half-mast for comic effect. A caricature of a nineteenth-century female temperance activist shouts: "Stop the celebration. That small boy is drunk." The adults are aghast, while the children scream, "Yeah, Bart!"

Bart appears on television with the caption "Drunken Boy—LIVE," and confronts the audience, asking "What are you lookin' at?" The scene cuts to the news anchor who says, "What are you looking at? The innocent words of a drunken child." The joke lies in the moderator's turn of phrase, Bart is certainly drunk, but not innocent. The drunk child in the scene transgresses ideals of white childhood innocence. We are accustomed to the optics of the vulnerable child in arguments for temperance—as one of the Prohibitionist women in the crowd shouts, "Will someone please think of the children?" Less familiar are scenes like this one that satirize how alcohol and childhood have been and continue to be used in political arguments about "family values," which is code for the white nuclear family. Some might argue that *The Simpsons* is not a "children's" show. On the contrary, from its release, the animated sitcom, like *MAD Magazine* before it, was "popular with youths of all ages," who embraced its satirical humor.[31] Indeed, the lessons of the drinking curriculum are best explored in popular texts like *The Simpsons* that on the surface are unlikely textbooks.

An extension of the temperance movement, the pedagogies of the drinking curriculum are highly visual and circulate broadly. Like *The Simpsons*, most of the texts examined in this book have (or had) mass appeal, making the visual a highly accessible pedagogical form. As comics scholar Hillary Chute argues, images are often the most conducive for communicating the unspeakable.[32] Likewise, images of drinking, drunkenness, and childhood contend with the volatile scenes and feelings that alcohol may evoke. This book's archive includes illustrated nineteenth-century temperance tracts, animated shorts, films, political cartoons, trade cards, stickers, public service announcements, advertisements, comics, and picture books. The list of texts examined here is not an exhaustive one, but rather a representative sampling. From the horrors of countless destitute, beaten, or murdered children in temperance fiction to the humor of drunk children on *Wacky Packages* bubble gum stickers, this dynamic set of visual texts of intoxication reveals how alcohol allows for the expression of contradictory feelings about childhood.

Lessons

I identify five overlapping lessons crucial to the ongoing cultural pedagogy of the drinking curriculum: D is for Drunkard; No Pets, No Drunks, No Children; Friends Don't Let Friends Drink and Drive; It's Funny When Kids Drink; and Mommy Needs a Cocktail. Though certainly not the only ones, these lessons best capture the paradoxical attachments to childhood that hide under the cover of educating or entertaining youth.

The first lesson, "D is for Drunkard" examines the image of the drunkard in children's literature from the first picture book, *The Orbis Pictus*, to the 2016 graphic novel *Louis Undercover*. Throughout the nineteenth century, the temperance movement used childhood to shift cultural understandings of alcohol from an innocuous and pleasurable part of everyday life to a dangerous and corrupting influence. Moving from the violence of temperance fiction, the next lesson "No Pets, No Drunks, No Children" examines intoxicated animals in animated cartoons, including characters Felix the Cat, Mickey Mouse, Dumbo, and the Drunk Stork. In the make-believe universe of animation, drunkenness fuels slapstick humor that provides a safe outlet for the expression of fears about rebellious children and childlike Others.

Bringing together the complementary pedagogies of fear and laughter discussed in the first two lessons, "Friends Don't Let Friends Drink and Drive" closely examines Steven Spielberg's 1982 blockbuster family film *E.T. the Extra-Terrestrial*.[33] In the movie, 10-year-old Elliott gets telekinetically drunk at school through the alien. This humorous intoxication scene circulates unremarkably alongside a growing cultural awareness about the horrors of drunk driving. That Elliott's tipsiness is played for laughs raises the question, when did drinking children become funny?

It feels irreverent to even make such a query, but it is the topic of the lesson, "It's Funny When Kids Drink." This lesson focuses on the visual humor of drinking and drunk children in comics, beginning with Bill Elder's spoofs on the beer industry in *MAD Magazine* in the 1950s followed by a consideration of *Wacky Packages* created by underground comix artists, including Art Spiegelman, Jay Lynch, and Bill Griffith. Extending this suspicion about childhood innocence, Lynda Barry uses gross-out drinking humor to walk a "funny/not-funny line" in her comics about girlhood, rape culture, and alcohol that will make some laugh and others turn away.[34]

The last lesson further pulls out the interwoven threads of violence and humor. "Mommy Needs a Cocktail" traces the legacies of the use of idealized white childhood innocence to sell alcohol as an antidote for the misery of motherhood. Specifically, intoxication—real or performed—sanctions an outpouring of maternal animosity through parodying, defacing, and repurposing cute children's commodities for laughs. This alcohol-infused humor is double-edged as it delights in the violence of child's play even as it infantilizes women through association with the diminutive accouterments of childhood. The book closes aptly, with a final exam that considers how the Covid-19 pandemic brought cultural ambivalence about alcohol and children back into the open in ways that require an understanding of the lessons of the drinking curriculum to fully comprehend.

Across time one enigmatic theme remains constant: while one adult hand reaches out to protect the child from alcohol, another one simultaneously invites her to take a sip. Examining different visual genres, from the overtly violent to the humorous, the moralistic to the profane, this book aims to understand what adults perform, value, and test when childhood, alcohol, and intoxication are pictured together. It offers an intervention into and, at times, an irreverent take on dominant protectionist paradigms that sanctify childhood as implicitly innocent. *The Drinking Curriculum* centers the paradoxical graphic narratives our culture uses to teach about alcohol, the roots of these pictorial tales in the nineteenth century, and the discursive hangover we nurse into the twenty-first.

Lesson One

D is for Drunkard

During the seventeenth and eighteenth centuries in the United States, alcoholic beverages were largely "regarded as good and healthy; alcohol was tonic, medicine, stimulant and relaxant. It was drunk at all hours of the day and night, by men and women of all social classes, and it was routinely given to children."[1] In *Drinking in America: Our Secret History*, Susan Cheever states that even in the 1820s "children drank before school, during school at recess, and after school," and that nineteenth-century elementary school pupils regularly started their day "with 'flip'—grain alcohol and fruit juice."[2] Alcohol was an everyday presence in the lives of many youth (such as the boy who loved rum discussed in the introduction to this book), who were taught to drink small amounts as babies to build up their tolerance to alcohol.[3] These examples of childhood drinking are flashpoints in a complex history of alcohol use and abuse in the United States. This first lesson chronicles how childhood and children's literature became a battleground upon which temperance reformers fought for abstinence.

While many Americans imbibed copious amounts of alcohol, others voiced concerns about U.S. drinking habits. In 1834 a temperance advocate warned that the United States "was fast becoming a nation of drunkards."[4] These worries were tied to new understandings of alcohol as harmful for the individual and for society. Beginning in the late eighteenth and early nineteenth centuries, excessive consumption of hard liquor came to be understood as a disease. Notably, in 1785, Benjamin Rush, Philadelphia physician and signer of the *Declaration of Independence*, published the pamphlet, *An Inquiry into the Effects of Ardent Spirits on the Human Body and Mind*.[5] He defined ardent spirits as distilled liquors. In a later edition Rush included "A Moral and Physical

Thermometer" on which beer and wine remained under the tenets of temperance and led to "cheerfulness, strength, and nourishment, when taken only in small quantities, and at meals." In contrast, "drams of Gin, Brandy and Rum in the morning" led to numerous vices like horse-racing and swearing as well as diseases, including inflamed eyes, red nose and face, sore and swelled legs, jaundice, dropsy, epilepsy, madness, and despair.[6] Beer and wine in moderation remained respectable. Rush discussed symptoms of acute and chronic drunkenness, and how the habitual overconsumption of hard liquor was a progressive disease; he also suggested a recovery model in which confirmed drunkards could go to a sober house for treatment. His tract medicalized alcohol abuse and "almost single-handedly launched the American temperance movement."[7]

Tied to broader crusades for abolition and suffrage that gained momentum in the 1830s and 1840s, temperance emerged out of Protestant churches in the United States. Advocates asked first for moderation, then abstinence, and, finally, largely through the efforts of the Anti-Saloon League, Prohibition through local, state, and national law. Temperance was also a global movement that is best understood as "a mutable and complex set of ideas, assumptions, rationales, and sources of identity, shaped and claimed by diverse, often competing groups and individuals over time, in different contexts, and for different purposes."[8] For example, Black reformers linked the liquor industry to predatory capitalism and slavery. It is often assumed that temperance activism was solely the purview of white evangelicals; however, Mark Lawrence Schrad argues that "nearly every major Black abolitionist and civil rights leader before World War I—from Frederick Douglass, Martin Delany and Sojourner Truth to F.E.W. Harper, Ida B. Wells, W.E.B. Du Bois, and Booker T. Washington—endorsed temperance and prohibition."[9] Similarly, Nazera Sadiq Wright demonstrates how temperance tales published in the Children's Department of the *Colored American* were interwoven with discourses of racial uplift and respectability.[10] Children's texts were a site of temperance activism and are an archive through which to view the medicalization of alcohol across the nineteenth century via the representation of the drunkard.

As a socializing mechanism, children's texts facilitate the circulation of meanings about drunkenness, visualizing cultural norms about who can get intoxicated, where, and how to act when drunk. Acceptable and unacceptable displays of inebriation are culturally bound, and from its inception, children's literature sought to teach its implied readers the moral ideal of temperance. Importantly, lessons about how to drink alcohol did not stand apart from the mainstream of children's literature; instead, they were fully incorporated into a genre highly adapted to cultural pedagogy. The first picture book for children, John Amos Comenius's *Orbis Sensualium Pictus* (*Visible World*), originally published in 1658 and released in the United States in 1810, aimed to make learning entertaining, and it was a "megahit in children's publishing" as well as a ground-breaking text within education.[11] The book centered on images and objects, arguing that children would learn to read through the senses. Pictorial literacy lessons in Latin, ABC's, and the natural world worked alongside moral education. Long considered a landmark text in education and children's literature, the *Orbis Pictus* is also a foundational visual primer within the drinking curriculum.

The *Orbis Pictus* includes instructional diagrams about making wine and brewing beer alongside other daily activities like baking bread. Most germane to this study, Comenius includes a chapter on "Temperance" within the moral philosophy section in which he advises the reader to prefer a mean to "meat *and* drink" and refrain desire "as with a bridle" (see Figure 7). The reasons to seek out moderation in alcohol consumption are fully illustrated. The numbered

Temperance. CXV. *Temperantia.*

Temperance, 1.	*Temperantia,* 1.
prescribeth a mean	præscribit *modum*
to Meat *and* Drink, 2.	*Cibo* & *Potui,* 2.
and restraineth the desire,	& continet *cupidinem,*
as with a Bridle, 3.	ceu *Freno,* 3.

Figure 7. "Temperance," John Amos Comenius, *Orbis Sensualium Pictus* (1658).

engraving pictures the trouble with intemperance for readers: when revelers are
made drunk (4.), they stumble (5.), spue (6.), and brabble (7.). Writes Comenius:
"From drunkenness proceeds lasciviousness from this a lewd life amongst
whoremasters (8.) and whores (9.) in kissing, touching, embracing, and dancing (10.)"[12] A vomiting man is pictured, and in the background, a prostitute
sits imbibing with a man. Socially defined meanings about drunkenness are
graphically coded, giving readers a lesson about temperance as both a moral
good and as a gendered behavior. Pleasure and indulgence are associated
with masculinity, whereas intoxicated women are pictured as "whores," a
visual pedagogy about drunkenness, femininity, and sexuality that continues
to stick. Alcohol, for men—its rightful imbibers—is not a demon or a poison;
rather, it is a beverage to enjoy in moderation. As the temperance movement
took hold, advocates doubled down on pathologizing alcohol, and drunken
comportment took on new meanings.[13]

Notably, as understandings of drinking went "from convivial to miserable,
sociable to antisocial, healthy to diseased" so, too, did images of drinking and
drunkenness in children's literature.[14] Karen Sánchez-Eppler notes that reformers focused especially on creating and circulating materials for children to
move the temperance message into the home where it would function as
"moral suasion to transform the public soul."[15] Drunkards were depicted in a
full range of materials from alphabet books to magic lantern slides to school
hygiene textbooks as activists worked to recruit a "cold water army" of youth.
For instance, in *A Was an Archer, or A New Amusing Alphabet For Children*
the popular rhyme reads: "A was an Archer, and Shot at a Frog, B was a Butcher
and kept a bull-dog, C was a Captain, all covered in lace, and D was a Drunkard and had a red face."[16] The drunkard appears alongside the archer, the
butcher, and the captain as an identity and as a mnemonic for the phonetic D
(see Figure 8). Children's texts reflect a broader cultural shift and negotiation of
ideas about alcohol consumption put forth via the temperance movement,
especially that alcohol is a poison, drinking a disease, and abstinence the
only cure.

As the pathologizing of drunkenness took hold in the nineteenth century,
education was viewed as "the wisest and most certain method of combating
intemperance."[17] Two graphic children's texts by physician Dr. Charles Jewett
provide an example of how these new connotations about drunkenness gained
purchase. In 1840 Jewett published *Temperance Toy* about the ills of drinking
set to the rhyme of "The House That Jack Built," writing in the introduction
that "it is not more a matter of regret than surprise that, among the multitude
of *picture-books* which are annually published, so few should have been got
up with a view to mingle with amusement, instructions in relation to the

Figure 8. "D is for Drunkard," from *A Was an Archer, or A New Amusing Alphabet For Children* (1836). Courtesy, American Antiquarian Society.

subject of temperance."[18] On the first page of *Temperance Toy* an inebriated man stands red-faced, smoking, in patched pants, with a bottle in his vest pocket. The red face and bulbous nose (often a signifier, "alcoholic's nose" or rhinophyma is due to an untreated skin condition, rosacea) code him as a drunkard. Visual markers like these reveal how "the interpretations people make of drinking, of the intoxicated state, and of behavior under intoxication are only partially shaped by the chemical or pharmacological effects of alcohol."[19] The text that accompanies the image reads, "Here is the man, whose bottle and can, are leading him down to perdition" (see Figure 9).[20] The bottle ushers the man to eternal damnation, and, as the illustration testifies, to disease and poverty in the here and now.

Similarly, Jewett's *The Youth's Temperance Lecturer* (1841), published the following year for older readers, also pictured drunkards as morally bankrupt and alcohol as a poison. In "The Beer Drunkard," an overweight man sits in a

Figure 9. Charles Jewett, *Temperance Toy* (1840).

chair with his swollen foot wrapped in a bandage and propped on a stool accompanied by a rhyme asking why men drink beer if it "swells up their face,
and makes them so lame they can't go" (see Figure 10).[21] As the temperance
movement morphed from moderation to abstinence, all alcohol, including
beer, was considered dangerous. Visual renderings of the physiological effects
of drinking communicate these culturally contingent understandings. Jewett
describes the beer drinker's blood as "poisoned," the face bloated, and the foot
so engorged by gout that he cannot walk without a crutch.

The Beer Drunkard.

Figure 10. Charles Jewett, *The Youth's Temperance Lecturer* (1841). Courtesy, Harvard Library.

The Youth's Temperance Lecturer also includes informational sections ranging from how alcoholic drinks are made to the wholesale trade of these beverages. Lessons about alcohol were also social messages because intoxication attacked sobriety, industriousness, and other white middle-class norms of masculinity. Temperance activists blamed social ills on those who sold intoxicating beverages like Albany Ale for profit as well as public drinking establishments such as the tavern in which the beer drinker sits.

In his introduction, Jewett warns that "No little boy or girl ever thought they should become a drunkard. You do not think so now, little reader, and yet you may be one, if your parents and yourself do not take great care to prevent it," and he argues that reading *The Youth's Temperance Lecturer* carefully alongside the right influences and God's blessing might save readers from the fate of the "drunkard's grave."[22] There is little doubt that the beer-drinking man is headed there as the easily recognizable trope of the drunkard was employed in visual temperance arguments about alcohol. Significantly, the man in the picture is not just intoxicated, he is addicted. The dangers of alcohol were medicalized and politicized, and that converged in visualizing temperance, equating personal and public health via road-to-ruin narratives.

The Road to Ruin

Visual texts were a crucial part of the nineteenth-century temperance movement's pedagogy, and, by the "1840s and early 1850s, temperance images were everywhere."[23] The idea of childhood became essential to graphic "road-to-ruin" narratives, in which one sip of liquor led to destitution, madness, and death, that circulated widely in the nineteenth century. Perhaps the most well-known cautionary graphic narrative is George Cruikshank's 1847 eight-plate series *The Bottle*. The first edition of *The Bottle* cost a shilling and sold more than 100,000 copies within a few days. Numerous dramatic adaptations, several poems, and a novel followed. *The Bottle* was exported to the United States, where, lacking copyright, it was quickly reproduced in texts like Timothy Shay Arthur's *Temperance Tales: or, Six Nights with the Washingtonians* with the images in some cases redrawn by other American artists mimicking Cruikshank's art without attribution.[24] Cruikshank is best known for his satirical political cartoons and his illustrations for Charles Dickens' novels, specifically *Sketches by Boz* and *Oliver Twist*. However, he was also a vocal teetotaler after giving up drink at the age of 55. Cruikshank had an intimate knowledge of alcohol abuse; his father, Isaac, died in a drinking contest, his brother was an alcoholic, and Cruikshank's own drinking habits were described as "phenomenal."[25]

The Bottle, like Nathaniel Currier's 1846 color lithograph *The Drunkard's Progress*, portrays how a drop of alcohol brings a man to madness and ruin. *The Bottle* foregrounds the child's well-being as the moral grounds on which adults should cease drinking. *The Bottle*'s visual sequence begins in a prosperous house, where three well-cared-for children with good clothes, shoes, toys, and food in the pantry dwell with their parents. When the father comes home with gin and suggests that the wife take "just a sip," the family unit quickly deteriorates. As the graphic narrative progresses, the father's alcohol abuse results in the death of the youngest child, and the remaining son and daughter must beg on the street. Ultimately, in a drunken rage, the man kills his wife with the bottle, "the instrument of all their misery," in front of his terrified children. The son is pictured dressed in rags with no shoes, a mirror of the father who spends the rest of his days in jail, "a hopeless maniac." Because the visual form compresses causality, sipping gin leads inexorably to chaos across less than half a dozen panels.

Cruikshank followed *The Bottle* with *The Drunkard's Children* in which he chronicles the fates of the son and daughter. It commences with the young siblings drinking in a gin shop, "neglected by their parents, educated only in

Figure 11. Plate 1, George Cruikshank, *The Drunkard's Children* (1848).

the streets, and falling into the hands of wretches who live upon the vices of others. They are led to the gin shop, to drink at that fountain which nourishes every species of crime" (see Figure 11). The rest of the plates picture the adolescent daughter and son as they move through a short life of dancing, gambling, dissipation, crime, imprisonment, and death.

The children's downfall is the result of their father's alcohol abuse, which concretizes addiction as a hereditary disease. The son dies of "early dissipation" on a convict ship and the "gin-mad" daughter commits suicide by throwing herself off a bridge. Cruikshank's *The Drunkard's Children* is important because it demonstrates how the road-to-ruin narrative relied on the child as a sympathetic victim and increasingly on childhood as a state that was easily corrupted. The visual link between popular understandings of alcohol as an addictive substance and childhood as a period of innocence underscores the precipitous decline that intoxication ushered in. Inevitable ruination was visually encoded in familiar images, repeated in other illustrations, and shared widely.

The road-to-ruin lesson was visually embedded enough in culture to begin to be standardized as part of the drinking curriculum, as seen in a January 1860 graphic narrative published in *The Youth's Temperance Advocate*. George Steady and Tom Wild start out together when they visit their Sunday School teacher (see Figure 12). However, after that, their paths diverge. Temperance

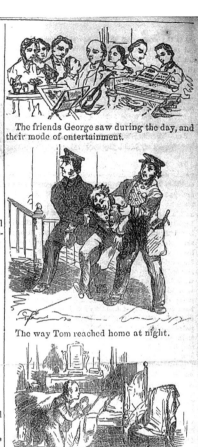

The friends George saw during the day, and their mode of entertainment.

First they call on their Sunday School Teacher and meet with a very pleasant reception.

The presents they received.

And how they were delighted with them and their visit.

How they kept together after the visit.

The acquaintances Tom called on and how they entertained him.

The way Tom reached home at night.

George terminates the day as good boys should, sober and with thankfulness to God.

Now is the time for new subscriptions for the ADVO-CATE. Fathers and Sunday School Teachers, if you want your children to be temperate, help them to the Advocate.

Will not ministers to whom we send this number exert themselves to introduce the ADVOCATE into their Sunday and day schools?

JUVENILE TEMPERANCE SPEAKER for Bands of Hope, Cadets, &c., now ready, for sale—price 25 cents.

Roll Books, Song Books, and Cards, of every description, for sale at this office.

Youth's Temperance Advocate, &c.

Published monthly, at the office of the *American Temperance Union*, No. 10, Park Bank, 5 Beekman Street, New York.

TERMS.

Single copy—for a year,	.	.	.	$0 25
Ten copies—to one address,		.	.	1 00
Fifty copies, do.,		.	.	4 50
One Hundred copies, do.,		.	.	9 00

TERMS BY MAIL, POST PAID.

Twenty-five copies—to one address,	.	.	$2 75
Fifty copies, do.,		.	.	5 60
One Hundred copies, do.,		.	.	11 00

Direct *Youth's Temperance Advocate*, No. 10 Park Bank. Payment always in advance. Continued till stopped by the subscriber.

Figure 12. *The Youth's Temperance Advocate* (1860).

boy George Steady "terminates the day as good boys should, sober and with thankfulness to God." In contrast, an inebriated Tom ends his night in the arms of two police officers. Too intoxicated to walk on his own, Tom's head lolls forward onto his chest, his eyes are at half mast, and his legs buckle. Tom's road to ruin begins as a youngster because of his bad individual choices and because he hails from a wine-drinking family. The young boy serves as a regulatory image for the white middle-class family. The drinking curriculum thus embedded not only the cautionary tale but modeled the benefits of its alternative, sobriety.

By the late-1800s these ideas were all but cemented in the public imagination. In T.S. Arthur's 1877 *Grappling with the Monster; Or, the Curse and the Cure of Strong Drink* a schoolboy takes a sip of liquor which leads to total wreckage in old age (see Figure 13).[26] Importantly, visual narratives about alcohol that commence with boyhood reflect a contemporaneous shift in the latter half of the nineteenth century to imagining childhood in material and visual culture as a state of white innocence and sentimentality.[27] Like the progression from childhood to adulthood, the drinker's demise is developmental.

The white male drunkard became emblematic of the temperance movement, and his downfall required childhood. The drunkard left innocence, pictured as fresh-faced boyhood, behind. The contrasting images of youthful promise and wretched decay emphasized corruption. This imagery, of course, also taught about race, class, and gender as addiction "was an implicitly white phenomenon."[28] Similarly, while female inebriates existed, they weren't usually shown in the road-to-ruin storylines, as "an upstanding young woman's choice to drink was much more difficult to excuse or empathize with than that of a young man. Most temperance advocates would have read it as a sign of preexisting immorality."[29] Following this logic, the daughter in Cruikshank's narrative, for instance, is also a prostitute. Marty Roth in *Drunk the Night Before* writes that it is not until the mid-nineteenth century that understandings of alcohol shifted from "a register of intoxication to one of addiction."[30] Making an important distinction between the two terms, Roth writes that "intoxication is an effect of drinking, addiction both is and is not."[31] Children's texts, often overlooked in social histories of drinking, document the medicalization of alcohol as well as the shift from drunkenness as a temporary state to the drunkard as an identity associated with disease and immorality.

BOYHOOD.
The First Step.

YOUTH.
The Second Step.

MANHOOD.
A Confirmed Drunkard.

OLD AGE.
A Total Wreck.

Figure 13. T.S. Arthur, *Grappling with the Monster—Or the Curse and the Cure of Strong Drink* (1877).

Disposable Children

Images of innocent children abused by drunk parents are a staple of temperance narratives. Anna Mae Duane argues that the suffering child's symbolic power rests in the "volatile combination of disarming vulnerability and unbearable suffering" that stakes a claim on the audience's empathy.[32] Intoxicated parents regularly subject innocent children to harm, including abject poverty, rape, beatings, hereditary addiction, and murder.[33] Jewett's *The Youth's Temperance Lecturer* includes a section entitled "effects of drunkenness" in which he gives "some account of what children are made to suffer whose parents become drunkards."[34] In one story, a father attacks his son. Jewett describes the scene for the reader (see Figure 14).

> Look at that hard-hearted man. He is holding his little boy by the hair with one hand, while the other is raised to give him a blow. And see that anxious mother, doing what she can to save her poor boy from the blow which is aimed at his head, while his little sister is running away in fright. Are they not all objects of pity? Thousands of children are beaten every day by intemperate parents.[35]

The suffering child is a casualty of the linked harm of patriarchy and alcohol. Small bodies are viciously punished in temperance fiction. Like other cautionary stories, temperance narratives "masquerade as educational tales but are in reality sadistic stories aimed at controlling behavior."[36] Yet, the temperance tale is distinct from other cautionary forms like the fairy tale in that children aren't punished for their misbehavior; the child is a disposable character to be violently mistreated in a lesson intended to remediate the drunken father. Thus, Jewett's book is different from the road-to-ruin narrative in that it is a multiform curriculum about a range of adult anxieties about control and loss of control.

Intoxication allows the abuse of a child, while acts of cruelty intoxicate the beholder. The beating of the young boy is left to the viewer's imagination and drunkenness is the spark that ignites readers to envision, delight in, and/or be repulsed by this violence. Karen Halttunen writes that Jewett's picture of torment was common for nineteenth-century reformers, who "assumed that the spectacle of pain was a source of illicit excitement, prurience, and obscenity—the power to evoke revulsion and disgust."[37] The image of the abused boy is, on one hand, a condemnation of intoxication. On the other, it is a voyeuristic scene of abjection and suffering that expresses hostility toward children. Jewett's work underscores how the visual archive of the drinking curriculum teaches us to see some things while others remain hidden. We have been taught to see

The Drunkard at home.

Figure 14. Charles Jewett, *The Youth's Temperance Lecturer* (1841). Courtesy, Harvard Library.

the suffering child as an exemplar of vulnerability that in turn upholds the myth of rational, caring adults. Yet, there are at least two visual lessons happening simultaneously through this image. The first results from the child's required viewing of violent illustrations to understand alcohol's dangers and the second from adults who consume visual images that depict or imply violence against children under the cover of moral instruction. This multi-generational pedagogy of harm was widely circulated through graphic temperance narratives.

The Women's Christian Temperance Union's hold on educating and assimilating children was officially in place by 1901 when "scientific temperance instruction," defined as the study of "the nature and effects of alcoholic drinks and other narcotics," became mandatory for U.S. schoolchildren for "nearly fifty years."[38] The establishment of abstinence education in public schools was one of the most powerful and insidious interventions of the temperance movement. Mary Hanchett Hunt, Julia Colman, and other WCTU members published textbooks like *Alcohol and Hygiene: An Elementary Lesson Book for Schools* in which alcohol was defined unequivocally as a liquid poison.[39] Like Jewett's *The Youth's Temperance Lecturer*, textbooks included diagrams and illustrations, as well as a set of review questions at the end of each chapter about the perils of alcohol consumption, such as: "How many persons every year die as drunkards?" For curious readers, the answer was over 60,000. Temperance ideologies were also woven into the widely circulated McGuffey Readers used for elementary literacy instruction.[40] The pictorial legacies of these lessons about addiction as a disease and abstinence as the cure carry over into the present.

Neo-Temperance Narratives

The idea that one sip of alcohol leads to ruin or rehab remains tenacious in the United States largely because of the hold of the temperance recovery group Alcoholics Anonymous started by Bill Wilson and Dr. Bob Smith in 1935. Philip McGowan contends that "maintaining that drinkers are genetically predisposed to the 'disease' of alcoholism, that one drink can unravel a successful life and lead to almost certain death, the imprint of nineteenth-century temperance remains long after the initial heat of its message abated."[41] In 1956 the American Medical Association officially classified alcoholism as an illness. In 2013, the inability to control the consumption of alcohol was redefined as alcohol use disorder (AUD), neither an illness, a disease, or a sin. Materials produced for the implied child reader evidence these shifting cultural definitions and demonstrate how imagery and ideas about addiction that emerged in the nineteenth century continue to circulate in more recent texts for youth.

Images of drunkards headed to perdition or propped up in taverns are no longer appropriate subjects for mainstream picture books, nor are images of abused or dead children. Addiction, if such imagery is portrayed visually at all, it is softened for young readers.[42] Visual discourses from the nineteenth century that frame alcoholism as a progressive disease and that chart a road to ruin are tempered to fit with contemporary ideas about childhood. Consider, for instance, 1983's *The Cat Who Drank Too Much*, written by Dr. LeClair Bissell and accompanied by photos by Richard Weatherwax. "Once upon a time there was a cat who drank too much. It started innocently enough—just a little with meals . . . But soon the cat was sneaking drinks when no one was looking."[43] The anthropomorphic cat replaces the explicit pictures of drunkards that peopled the pages of nineteenth-century literature (see Figure 15). Unquenchable thirst serves as a metaphor for alcoholism.

The cat's descent into addiction is a tragicomedy, presented through a series of documentary-style black-and-white photos in which he becomes obsessed with drinking, experiences personality changes, sees and hears things that aren't there, and passes out in the middle of the afternoon. Finally, like the drunkards in temperance texts, "his appearance deteriorated . . . glassy-eyed, wet furred,

His appearance deteriorated . . . glassy-eyed,
wet furred, hopeless looking.

Figure 15. Dr. LeClair Bissell and Richard Weatherwax, *The Cat Who Drank Too Much* (1983).

hopeless looking." After the cat gets so low that he contemplates suicide, he goes to an Alcoholics Anonymous treatment center. The tenets of the temperance branch of the drinking curriculum are evident here with one sip of alcohol leading to the cat's addiction and then to a recovery house.

The award-winning 2016 graphic novel for young readers, *Louis Undercover* written by Fanny Britt and illustrated by Isabelle Arsenault follows a similar recovery plot.[44] The comic is narrated and visualized from the perspective of 11-year-old Louis about his father's alcohol use disorder. Louis narrates the book, which begins: "My dad cries." The "undercover" in the title captures how Louis spies on his father. A singular teardrop, drawn in a muted palette, symbolizes the enormity of the dad's sadness. The hand-lettered text further emphasizes Louis' perspective and forges an intimacy with the reader: "Between you, me and the bus driver, you don't need to be a rocket scientist to know that if my dad cries, it's first and foremost because of the wine."[45] Louis describes the physical toll drinking takes on his father, who begins imbibing every morning at 11:00. Codes of addiction set up in nineteenth-century visual temperance culture are reproduced here, including shaking hands, drinking alone, passing out surrounded by bottles, and the signature shaded bulbous nose (see Figure 16).

Alcohol and drunkenness continue to portray a threat to the white middle-class by positioning women and children, especially young boys, as vulnerable subjects. At the story's climax, the family finds the father passed out drunk on a park bench, a large black cloud emanating from his mouth as the last bit of liquid blue tips out of a bottle. On the double-page spread, the mother and sons stand on one side of the image separated from the father in a scene that recalls any number of destitute mothers and their children at the end of a road-to-ruin narrative. Similarly, the idea that alcoholism is hereditary finds purchase in *Louis Undercover*. On the steps of the treatment facility, father and son make eye contact and Louis contemplates his shared biology. "What I see in his eyes right then, something like an earthquake or a drowning, makes me think that I might have to be like him and drink all kinds of wine to forget."[46] The linkage of the drunk father–vulnerable son is a nineteenth-century temperance trope that reinforces alcohol's harm to white masculinity even as it critiques alcoholism.[47] This emphasis on male drinking as the problem is also underscored by the lingering cultural lesson that it is the wife's job to "maintain the family morally and emotionally."[48] Like earlier graphic narratives, *Louis Undercover* reinforces white masculinity even as temperance discourse uses the figure of the child to critique the patriarchal intransigence and abuse (to different degrees) that keep women and children bound—in any case—either to the violence of the alcoholic or the presumed rationality of the father who abstains.

Louis Undercover spotlights the individual and his recovery and alcohol use as a disorder to be fixed or managed. The book sympathizes with the father's struggle, and the graphic physical violence in tales like *The Youth's Temperance Lecturer* is erased in favor of a story about the psychological effects of addiction on a child. On the other hand, *Louis Undercover* ultimately recycles visual temperance tropes that emerge out of nineteenth-century medical models, and in turn folds into a newer neo-liberal context of self-help and recovery in the twenty-first century, a $35 billion-per-year industry in the United States.[49]

The D is for Drunkard lesson of the drinking curriculum contains both truth and fiction: drinking alcohol doesn't necessarily lead to abject poverty or death or gout; and likewise sobriety doesn't always result in wellness, success, or good citizenship. Images of the drunkard are interpretive devices that make visible cultural meanings about intoxication. Addiction is a social and medical issue that continues to be reproduced through familiar pictures and scripts, even as no single theory "be it pharmacological, psychological, sociological, or anthropological, is capable of explaining more than a small

Figure 16. Fanny Britt and Isabelle Arsenault, *Louis Undercover* (2016). *Undercover* reproduced with permission from Groundwood Books Limited, Toronto. Text copyright © 2017 by Fanny Britt, illustrations copyright © 2017 by Isabelle Arsenault. www.groundwoodbooks.com. English Translation Reproduced by Permission of Walker Books Ltd, London, SE11 5HJ. www.walker.co.uk.

proportion of the numerous interpretations made."[50] Picturing drunkards as cautionary figures in graphic narratives explicitly for youth went out of fashion; however, temperance lessons provided a catalog of images and behaviors that would become a cultural storehouse of sight gags for comic representation. The next lesson, "No Pets, No Drunks, No Children" focuses on how cartoons teach about intoxication through humor, the other side of the violence coin.

Lesson Two
No Pets, No Drunks, No Children

A 1951 rental listing in *The Tampa Tribune* March 15, 1951, reads "SMALL home, modern, for rent, on Linebaugh and Laura, unfurn. No pets, no drunks, no children."[1] One of countless ads in newspapers of the era, the landlord lumps children, animals, and drunks together as equally unsuitable tenants. This grouping is less incongruous than it first appears. In a 1913 article, "A Study of Fourteen Cases of Alcoholism in Children Apparently Free from Morbid Heredity," physician Alfred Gordon observed that from "many standpoints" the child "could be compared to an animal. Like the latter, he is attracted only by things that appeal to his tastes. As reasoning power is rudimentary, impulses cannot yet be controlled. The child is very anxious to possess what appeals to him and displays violent anger when his desire is not promptly satisfied."[2] According to Dr. Gordon, a child's animalistic impulsiveness left to grow without education and adult guidance makes "acquired alcoholism" highly likely. Gordon, like the landlord, naturalizes intemperance as the defining characteristic of children, animals, and drunks; each has the potential to lose control, and in the process, transgress social conventions and rules of bodily comportment. Pets are often treated as surrogate children, children are sometimes treated like animals, and drunks are regularly compared to both. The vulnerability of the child, the intoxicated, and the pet also makes them targets of laughter. These troublemakers coalesce in the slapstick universe of animation as drunken animals are routinely subjected to violence.

While ideas associated with the child—impulsiveness, anger, lack of understanding, vulnerability, and disobedience—are important for understanding the cultural work of cartoon intoxication, most of the animated shorts discussed below were not created solely for children. Though easy associations are often made between animation and childhood, Peter Kunze reminds us that cartoons like "Betty Boop, Bugs Bunny, and Tom and Jerry—had broad appeal, and the themes, humor, and even cultural allusions suggest a desire to placate adult and child audiences alike"; many of the shorts that enjoyed large multi-age audiences were later repackaged as "children's culture" on Saturday morning television.[3] Additionally, young viewers consume materials not intended for them (one reason why efforts in the post-WWII era to curtail alcohol advertising on television failed).[4] Thus this lesson does not concern itself with the implied child viewer but rather focuses on how childhood, defined as a state of physical and intellectual vulnerability, informs depictions of intoxication that sanction and make comedic violence legible.

Punch Drunk: Comedic Violence and Intoxication

Animated shorts depict the mayhem of boozing as gleeful, even celebratory for audience and animated characters alike, through the highly visual form of slapstick humor. The physical comedy of slapstick relies on excessive, continuous, and often violent assaults on the body. "Faces are hit by pies, bodies suffer slaps and blows, they tumble, fall, collapse, are dropped, ejected, or thrown from cars or trains at full speed, are run over by buses and knocked down by fists, bricks, frying pans, or mallets."[5] For example, when Felix the Cat goes to the Whoopee Club in Otto Messmer's 1928 animated short "Woos Whoopee" he drinks beer and liquor, dances with cats that are not his wife, and drives drunk. His inebriated body is malleable: in a hat's off move he removes his ears and bows, curls himself into a ball, and hurtles out of the frame; in a moment of fear his feet leave his torso hanging in the air, and he's eaten by a fish that turns into a musical horn with a feathered tail. The short includes hallucinations—first a dancing lamppost then elephants, snakes, and finally a crude alien monster. Intoxication triggers the attacks on Felix's body. Yet, the cat grins after a scare, and his alcohol consumption results in "pleasure for pleasure's sake."[6] Humor and violence co-exist in the childish antics of drunken characters without consequence.

The state of intoxication fits hand in glove with the physical violence of slapstick. The resulting laughter is aimed at the characters' foibles and often their humiliation. Comedic violence captures anxieties about embodiment, evoking laughter from linking improbable physical states (e.g., your ears don't come off when you take your hat off) to all too familiar feelings of out-of-control bodies and emotions. Journalist Sarah Baird observes that "from the first time moving illustrations merged with sound during the 'golden age' of animation in the late 1920s, drinking quickly became as classic a cartoon trope as slipping on a banana peel."[7] Certainly as a form, animation allows a "greater latitude for violent transformation."[8] Theorizing early Mickey Mouse shorts, Walter Benjamin writes that animation ushered in new and frightening ways of thinking about the body's vulnerability, noting that "we see for the first time that it is possible to have one's own arm, even one's own body, stolen."[9] So, too, when intoxicated, the body is not one's own—it may stagger, fall, tip over, and vomit. Felix the Cat suggests that drunkenness might be both scary and pleasurable. On one level, animated drunken animals poke fun at inebriation as inglorious, and on another demonstrate a desire to experience what it feels like to exist in an altered state.

Intoxicated Mice and Pink Elephants

Created during Prohibition in the United States during the 1920s, animated shorts like "Woos Whoopee," crystallized intoxicated characters as subjects of violence (both vulnerable to it and capable of inflicting it) and humor.[10] Similarly, one of Walt Disney and Ub Iwerks' early Mickey Mouse cartoons also used drunkenness as entertainment. The release of *Gallopin' Gaucho* (1928), a parody of Douglas Fairbanks' 1927 film *The Gaucho*, followed on the heels of the first successful Mickey Mouse sound cartoon, *Steamboat Willy* (1928). In *Gallopin' Gaucho*, Mickey Mouse travels through Argentina on his trusty rhea (a large flightless bird) and stops for a drink at the Cantino Argentino, where he kicks off his boot to light a cigarette and uses his tail to pick up a mug full of beer (see Figure 17). Beer foam replaces the traditional pie in the face, and to remove it Mickey sticks out an unbelievably long tongue to lick bubbles off his forehead and all around his face, sweeping it clean.

Importantly, the beer, like the cigarette, is one of Mickey's masculine accouterments and he drinks without getting intoxicated. He can hold his liquor in ways that boost his heterosexual bravado as he aggressively tries to woo Minnie Mouse and fend off Black Pete. In contrast, his rhea gets completely soused. When Mickey needs him to chase his rival, the crapulous bird reports drunk for duty. Weaving toward Mickey, Carl Stalling's musical underscoring—a slackened version of "For He's a Jolly Good Fellow"—exaggerates the humor of the bird's unsteady gait. The rhea holds a beer stein and it hiccups and tries to walk on legs that bend at all angles. The bird's intoxicated ungainliness is the audience's fodder for laughter. The visual storytelling is quick, underscoring how "slapstick laughter plays on the spectator's insensitivity by allowing no time for healing or commiserating, submitting the character to a deliberately excessive and constant assault."[11] Its body repeatedly assaulted, the bird and its legs twist into knots, crumpling in a circular heap only to stand again for

Figure 17. "Gallopin' Gaucho" (1928). Walt Disney Productions.

more abuse. The consumption of alcohol enhances Mickey Mouse's swagger, yet when the rhea gets into its cups, laughter ensues. Indeed, the mouse's time as a drinker was short-lived. By 1931, a writer for *Time* wrote that "already censors have dealt sternly with Mickey Mouse. He and his associates do not drink, smoke or caper suggestively."[12] By 1933 Disney distributed its *Mickey Mouse Magazine* through dairy companies and the mouse became associated with the more wholesome beverage, milk.[13]

Indeed, abstention from or the consumption of alcohol establishes hierarchies. The drunken rhea plays child to Mickey's adult, an association furthered when the bird emerges from the family room of the cantina. Similarly, in the 1936 Oscar-award-winning Silly Symphony short, *The Country Cousin*, animated by Art Babbitt and Les Clark, social class is marked via intoxication. Based on Aesop's "The Town Mouse and The Country Mouse," Morty Citymouse invites his "hick" cousin "Abner Countrymouse" to join him in the city to live in splendor. While the short relies on the fable for meaning, it is also a master class in drunk slapstick visual humor. Dressed in overalls, Abner misses his upper-crust cousin's social cues. While Morty eats tiny bites of cheese,

Abner gorges himself. When Abner's face catches on fire after eating mustard, he plunks it into a giant champagne coupe. Smitten with drink, and as another example of his unbridled appetite, Abner drinks more, then hiccups, lounges in the glass, and sucks up the dregs of the bubbles from the glass stem. For the remainder of the musical short, Abner's drunkenness drives not only the plot but innovative animation techniques that play with the malleability of the body. Abner lounges in the coupe, slips and slides to get out of the glass, and hallucinates three Morty Citymice. At the climax, Abner, filled with liquid courage, kicks the house cat, which results in cascading slapstick violence, including an electrical shock when the mouse tries to hide in a socket, a dramatic chase through the city from Abner's point of view in which human feet, roller skates, and a horn with a tail all threaten him as he attempts to return to the country.[14]

The intemperate behaviors of animated animals, like Abner, Mickey's rhea, and Felix the Cat, evoke associations with childishness in ways that safely mediate fears of and anxieties about vulnerable Others. The fusing together of childishness, animalistic instincts, and drunkenness as traits to be condoned and contained, managed by violence and laughter, can be read as anxieties around both individual bodies and childlike Others within the larger social fabric of the United States. In *Birth of an Industry*, Nicholas Sammond argues that laughter and brutality are a signature of American animation's racist roots. Cartoon characters, including Mickey Mouse, exist as "vestigial minstrels" that extend the performative legacies of blackface minstrelsy, prompting Sammond to ask how when "faced with such horrific violence and fierce torment, we are amused, tickled, jollified."[15] The legibility of this comedic harm also relies on the construct of childhood, which as Anna Mae Duane has deftly argued, is a rhetorical device that has long been "deployed to disempower various Others."[16] Racialized and non-normative bodies have been and continue to be dehumanized as childlike. In visual culture, animosity expresses itself through the juvenile, the silly, and the unruly. Disney's 1941 *Dumbo* exemplifies how intoxication's temporality fuels and excuses these ambivalences.

Dumbo was based on the 1939 roll-a-book entitled *Dumbo the Flying Elephant* written by Helen Aberson and illustrated by Harold Pearl.[17] The book and movie have an alcohol-infused backstory. In the film, a uniformed stork voiced by Sterling Price Holloway, Jr. delivers a baby elephant named Jumbo to its mother. The name refers to the real-life Jumbo, an alcohol-addicted elephant, and the "children's giant pet" that nineteenth-century entertainer and temperance activist P.T. Barnum bought from the London Zoo in 1882 to exhibit in his traveling North American circus. The pachyderm was given

Figure 18. *Dumbo* (1941). Walt Disney Productions.

massive amounts of alcohol to keep him under control and "would knock down a bottle of champagne or whisky."[18] Like Jumbo, Dumbo also imbibes champagne in one of the drinking curriculum's most remarkable lessons.

When Dumbo returns from visiting his imprisoned mother, he is bereft. Trying to console him, Timothy Q. Mouse instructs the elephant to take a trunk full of water from a tub into which the hard-partying circus clowns in their haste to "hit the big boss" up for a raise (a reference to the strike going on between animators and Walt Disney) have knocked a bottle of champagne, turning the liquid to a brightly toxic bubbly green. Dumbo complies and after his first drink hiccups as bubbles flow out of his nose. He then loses control of his body and slides down the side of the tub. Dumbo's face underscores his surprise at the mishap as the alcohol takes over (see Figure 18).

The scene owes much to *The Country Cousin*—both the inadvertent intoxication that begins with humor and ends with terror and Timothy Q. Mouse's drunken antics.[19] After falling into the bucket, the rodent hiccups and then begins to sing as the champagne-infused water goes to his head. Slapstick play ensues and the mouse walks with an unsteady gait and then elatedly floats in and on champagne bubbles. Elephant and mouse share a pleasurable tipsiness that abruptly ends when Dumbo blows a bubble in the shape of a cube, which signals the beginning of the nightmarish "Pink Elephants on Parade" sequence.

Dumbo remains "the high-water mark of pink elephants in pop culture."[20] Pink elephants, like snakes in one's boots, are a euphemism for delirium tremens, the visual symptoms that accompany withdrawal from alcohol addiction. This altered state has long been fodder for humor. In his novel *John Barleycorn*, Jack London suggests that these kinds of drinkers who see pink elephants are the object of ridicule in "the funny papers"; they are also the butt of jokes in popular culture.[21] So, too, Dumbo's inadvertent intoxication is meant to evoke laughter.

Animated by Hicks Lokey and Howard Swift and directed by Norman Ferguson, the sequence's visuals shift quickly from a three-dimensional background to a flat black surface.[22] The elephants break the fourth wall. Norman Klein links the "Pink Elephants" scene in *Dumbo* to earlier animated portrayals of drunkenness like Felix the Cat's discussed earlier, writing that:

> Rules about how to draw drunkenness had been set up fairly standardly in the twenties throughout the cartoon industry. The drunk was usually shown inside a nightmare, with lots of spinning and loss of balance. Often it was a whimsical hell, and this was still the rule in cartoons made in the forties, like Dumbo's dream of pink elephants: lines metamorphose into spectral volumes.[23]

A frightened Timothy Q. Mouse spends most of the time under Dumbo's cap while the menacing "Pink Elephants on Parade" performed by The Sportsman plays.[24] The lyrics add to the harrowing landscape as "in both its words and its images, the song teeters between dream and nightmare, whimsy and paranoid terror."[25] To be sure, the shape-shifting technicolor pachyderms that Dumbo and Timothy Q. Mouse see are simultaneously fascinating and terrifying and the spectacle induces laughter and fear.

Elephant and mouse awake from their shared delirium, clear-eyed and sober, in a tree in one of the Disney Company's most racist scenes with a group of crows, led by Jim Crow and voiced by white actor Cliff Edwards. Sammond argues that in animated cartoons, including *Dumbo*, "humor gained some of its affective charge not in spite of . . . racism but *because* of it."[26] To that end, drunkenness ushers Dumbo into proximity to Blackness vivifying an animalistic, dehumanizing, and racializing matrix that relies on animated cuteness for cover. Specifically, intemperance codes characters as childlike; as vulnerable and unpredictable when under the influence; and, in need of protection and policing. This childish status makes Dumbo, Timothy Q. Mouse, and the flock of crows legible in the drinking curriculum because animals, drunks, and children perform the audience's desire for transitory unruliness and its suppression.

At heart, *Dumbo* is a tale of violence aimed at an unprotected, young creature. As one critic commented, for forty of the sixty-four minutes of the film "the writers have at this baby elephant and his mother with a sadism that would give pause in the offices of the Brothers Grimm."[27] This is a story of forced abandonment in which the baby Dumbo is taunted, tortured, and almost killed by the circus clowns in a high-diving trick. The presence of both horror and humor evoked by intoxication predictably relies on slapstick to excavate a continuum of feelings from sympathy to fear to mirth. Thus, like other texts in the drinking curriculum, the presence of the childish exaggerates the effects of intoxication for humorous or cautionary effects. In *Dumbo* the audience laughs at the transgression of innocence, and because it occurs within the make-believe space of animation, it provides a seemingly benign context within which to express aggression.

About Timothy Q. Mouse and Dumbo, a critic for *The New York Times* observes that "together chance leads them to imbibe a tub of diluted champagne, and out of this fortunate accident Dumbo discovers that he can fly."[28] Defining the child proxy's inadvertent drunkenness as a "fortunate accident" shows the morphing contours of childhood as a category in relationship to alcohol. Intoxication is not an inherent evil and the reviewer expresses no concern over child viewers taking up drinking because of what they have seen. Rather, inebriation reveals Dumbo's unique talents. Drunkenness stirs up pleasure and fear, and it is the outlet through which Dumbo learns that he can fly. Analyzing this film as part of the drinking curriculum reveals a broader history of animation in which scenes of intoxication are also scenes of innovation and experimentation, played for laughs—entertaining interludes for both adults and children. About the enticements of Disney's early animated shorts, Esther Leslie writes that

> [t]his was not just children's stuff, and certainly not sugar-sweet. Whether they were for adults or children was indeterminate. They were simply for anarchists of any age.
>
> Cartoons, for all of their slapstick playing, seemed to appeal to intellect and imagination.[29]

Slapstick humor makes palatable Dumbo's mistreatment, including an episode of inadvertent drunkenness that leads him through a hellscape of shapeshifting, singing pink elephants.

Reading *Dumbo* as an alcohol narrative flummoxes some contemporary viewers because of the foregone conclusion that Disney products are wholesome fare for impressionable youth. For instance, Practical Folks' Drunk Disney "the show where a bunch of childless 20-somethings get drunk and tell you what the movie of the week teaches children" are simultaneously aghast and entertained by the drunken pink elephant scene in *Dumbo*.[30] Yet, we should not be surprised. The trouble here is not with Disney or with representations of drinking but rather with the myth of childhood innocence. Walt Disney himself created a persona for public consumption, stating, "I'm not Walt Disney. I do a lot of things Walt Disney wouldn't. Walt Disney doesn't smoke. I smoke. Walt Disney doesn't drink. I drink."[31] Similarly, beneath the Disney company's veneer of innocence lie numerous scenes of drinking including Mickey Mouse's early appearances as well as in G-rated animal films like *The Aristocats* or *The Great Mouse Detective* in "entertaining, comical, and enticing ways."[32] In *Dumbo* intoxication exposes innocence as both a state to protect and a taint.

The Drunk Stork

Warner Bros.' Drunk Stork shares with the rhea in *Gallopin' Gaucho* a penchant for reporting blotto for duty. One in a fleet of birds, Drunk Stork, number 672 was created by Bob Clampett and Friz Freleng and voiced by Mel Blanc. The bird appeared in six episodes from 1946 to 1959 and has been described as a character that "could drink Foster Brooks under the table."[33] In contrast to the earnest stork in *Dumbo* or the idealized birds on greeting cards that deliver little bundles of joy to eager parents, this bird has little regard for babies. The first cartoon to feature the character, "Baby Bottleneck" (1946) begins with a narrator reading a headline in the news "Unprecedented demand for babies overworks stork!" As the camera pans down the frame, we see the bird laid out alongside shot glasses and bottles; he has literally drunk himself under the table. Relegated to the floor of Manhattan's most prestigious nightclub, the Stork Club, the bird expresses his exhaustion by drinking himself into a stupor. Taking on the speech mannerisms of Jimmy Durante, the Drunk Stork expresses the lack of appreciation shown to him: "I'm mortified. I'm disgustipated. I do all the work and the fathers get all the credit." The Drunk Stork's resentments about overwork during this first year of the U.S. Baby Boom underscores a broad cultural ambivalence about children cloaked in humor that is a hallmark of cartoons in which this character appears.

The Drunk Stork is regularly so inebriated that he delivers infants into the hands of the wrong parents, subjecting the unknowing parcels to all sorts of potential harm. When the Drunk Stork mistakenly delivers a baby mouse to

Sylvester the Cat in the 1953 "A Mouse Divided," the cat grabs a cleaver, asking Mrs. Sylvester to choose "heads or tails." When the tiny baby mouse calls him "daddy," Sylvester has a change of heart and spends the rest of the episode protecting him through violent physical gags from predatory cats who wish to eat his "offspring."[34] The incongruous parent-child duos result in exaggerated threats to and make-believe violence that surround the helpless, unknowing baby.

The Drunk Stork plays the role of fool, buffoon, and prankster. Like other fools, the bird's role is to "tickle, coax and cajole their supposed betters into truth, or something akin to it."[35] He speaks truths after drinking outrageous amounts of champagne with parents of newborns, often behind closed doors. In the 1955 "Stork Naked" the bird enters an apartment sober and exits visibly inebriated, stating that "one thing about this job [hiccup], everyone is always glad to see the stork." The truth is that everyone may be happy to see the stork, but not necessarily the crying baby.

Animated shorts that feature the Drunk Stork distill parental fears and anxieties, which are the object of satire in the 1954 "Goo Goo Goliath." Narrated by Norman Nesbitt, the mockumentary parodies parenting manuals, especially Dr. Spock's revolutionary advice for raising children made popular in his 1946 manual, *The Common Sense Book of Baby and Child Care.* The cartoon begins with elegant storks carrying tidy baby bundles into and out of the Stork, Inc. building. A voice-over informs viewers that "through the ages, the stork has been symbolically represented as the bird that delivers newborn babes to their future homes. The storks are jealously proud." The sound of the Drunk Stork guffawing disrupts the romanticized scene. And, in a visual counterpoint to this sentimentalized image, the inebriated bird sits, legs stretched out and completely hammered on a couch, his blue delivery hat askew, and bloodshot eyes at half-mast. The Drunk Stork explains his exploits to an unimpressed colleague through hiccups and slurred speech.

> Oh brother what a party that last delivery. Their first baby. Champagne all over the place. All buckets of it. I tried to break away, heaven knows but no dice. It was give the stork another one. One for the road.

When an announcement plays over the loudspeaker: Calling stork 672, the Drunk Stork replies: "Hey that's my number 549. Yes, sir 321 coming up." The bird who cannot even remember his employee number remains tasked with delivering a baby to Mrs. Giant at the top of the beanstalk.

While the other storks fly off elegantly through the air with their bundle accompanied by victorious music, the Drunk Stork plummets out of the frame to the sound of a sputtering plane engine. The animators' gags rely on the incongruity between the Drunk Stork's disheveled appearance and un-graceful comportment with the elegant and dutiful birds that usually deliver these most precious packages. Inebriated, the bird continues struggling to carry the heavy bundle. His descent takes place outside of the frame and the next scene opens with the bird leaning on a lamppost, his baby parcel a few steps away from him on the ground (see Figure 19).

> The Drunk Stork: Let's face it. I can't fly any further. Let's see where is it supposed to go? Well that's prepost . . . ridiculous. I couldn't get this load up to a dandelion. I've got to deliver this load someplace. And this place looks as good as any. Never saw a house yet where a baby wasn't welcome.

Too sloshed to fly up the beanstalk, the stork delivers Mrs. Giant's baby to un-suspecting human parents, Ethel and John. The short pokes fun at Dr. Spock's advice: "Don't be afraid to trust your own common sense." The mother uses the swimming pool to bathe her tot and much to the father's outrage gives the baby his new white sidewall car tires as a teething toy. As the usual childish objects are replaced with things that are assuredly not common sense, the

Figure 19. "Goo Goo Goliath" (1954). Warner Bros. Merry Melodies.

cartoon suggests that these intensive attempts to please and nurture the child are folly.

The gap between parenting advice and the child's behavior widens for humorous effect. "A well-trained child can be taught to be helpful around the house" advises the voice-over when the giant baby tosses his petrified father in a car through the air to his office. The narrator tells the viewer that "in spite of all vigilance, children will usually take advantage of a careless moment, such as a gate left thoughtlessly open and a baby innocently wanders away" at which point the distracted parents fail to notice that their 42-foot baby has left the yard. The giant infant walks the streets of Los Angeles, where he lifts and puts the iconic Brown Derby restaurant roof on his head, leaving the tiny adult diners exposed and panicked (see Figure 20). The Drunk Stork has unleashed a baby monster, and the short's humor lies in transgressing categories—the child, not the adult, is in control.

"Goo Goo Goliath" gives expression to ambivalence about child-rearing, showing how the arrival of a baby wreaks havoc on routines and picturing the chilling possibilities of child rule. The stork finds the giant infant sleeping in the arm of the Statue of Liberty and deduces that he has given the giant at the top of the beanstalk a human baby; the shot focuses in on the incongruity of a large giant trying his best to diaper (and not inadvertently harm) the small child

Figure 20. "Goo Goo Goliath" (1954). Warner Bros. Merry Melodies.

in his care. After retrieving the correct baby, the Drunk Stork takes over the narration, stating that "things are straightened out." The short ends with a suburban red house, yet when the camera pans out, the stork has left the human infant at the zoo with a kangaroo, the baby sitting in a doe's pouch. The Drunk Stork *in vino veritas* delivers a comedic truth: the most well-meaning and affluent parents are not in control. Never preoccupied about the child in his care, the Drunk Stork's inebriation is doubled down on by the animators to emphasize his clownishness, shrouding an animosity about children. In contrast to *Dumbo*, in which aggression hides under the cloak of cuteness, Warner Bros. expresses the fears and anxieties of parenting through the drunken fool.

Tiny Toons

This history provides context for a turning point in the drinking curriculum via a controversy that featured intoxicated animated animals in a show intended for children. Steven Spielberg's Emmy-award-winning *Tiny Toons Adventures* was a collaboration between Amblin Entertainment and Warner Bros. that aired from 1990 to 1992. The series rebooted the original Looney Tunes/Merry Melodies characters produced by Warner Bros. specifically for children's television. The show, like the original Looney Tunes cartoons, relies on slapstick violence for humor. The reboot features teen characters Buster Bunny, Plucky Duck, and Hamton J. Pig, who attend Acme Looniversity and are taught lessons by classic characters, including Bugs Bunny and Daffy Duck.

The show came under fire in 1991 for Episode number 68, "Elephant Issues" (a play on Relevant Issues) and a cartoon segment entitled "One Beer."[36] In the controversial short, Buster Bunny, Plucky Duck, and Hamton J. Pig find a bottle of beer in the fridge. Buster Bunny's face comes into the frame, beer bottles replace his pupils as he asks: "What'll it be boys? Juice? Milk? Soda? Or a cold one?" Buster Bunny then grows green devil horns and with a malicious expression and employing satirical humor states, "In this episode, we're showing the evils of alcohol." After the characters drink the beer, they engage in a fifteen-second burping montage. There is the predictable play with bubbles, hiccups, and beer spewing. Once drunk, the animators code this loss of innocence as the characters switch from sweet-faced youngsters to drunken sots. Plucky Duck, Hamton J. Pig, and Buster Bunny appear in adult clothes, and sport stubble, a reversal of familiar visuals in which a drunk man is made childish (see Figure 21).

The characters steal a police car and as they speed through the streets with Plucky at the wheel the following conversation, meant to be darkly comedic, ensues.

Figure 21. "One Beer" (1991). Warner Bros. / Amblin Entertainment.

BUSTER BUNNY: So Plucky . . . (pausing to drink from the beer
    bottle) . . . how does it feel to be D.W.I.?
PLUCKY DUCK: D.W.I., what's that? (takes a drink from the bottle)
BUSTER BUNNY: (Slurring his speech) D.W.I., driving while intoxicated.
PLUCKY DUCK: Well, that's ridiculous, I don't know how to drive.

Ultimately, the car careens off a cliff and smashes to the ground next to a head-stone that reads RIP. The offending beer bottle pops out of the car and wiggles to the front of the frame. Escorted by a lullaby, the three characters float out of the car with halos and angel wings into the sky. As they do, they shed their robes and halos, and break the fourth wall.

"I hope the kids got the message."

"Yeah, drinkin's uncool."

"So, do we get to do a funny episode tomorrow? I hope so."

The episode aired only once and was held from syndication because of its depiction of intoxication and "reckless behavior," including drunk driving.[37] Concerned adults complained that "One Beer" "was either too dark for children and/or made too much light of alcoholism" and "it was pulled from reruns for almost two decades."[38]

This concern for an imagined child viewership occluded how generations of youth had been educated in drinking humor through earlier Warner Bros. cartoons that had been repackaged as children's fare as Saturday morning cartoons. By the time "One Beer" aired, the 1990 Children's Television Act had passed, aiming to make television less commercial and more educational, the result of decades of activism to censor what youth viewed.[39] Yet, "One Beer" *was* children's television programming. The animators and scriptwriters refused protectionist discourses, and instead satirized decades of adult panics over the content of children's texts. They refused to moralize about drinking and about childhood as a state of common-sense innocence. While audiences of any age could watch Felix drunk driving and laugh at the Drunk Stork's inability to fly straight with an infant in tow with impunity, the same trope is no longer available by 1990. Another context for understanding why the hallmark comedic violence of earlier Warner Bros. recycled in the subversive "One Beer" fell flat included public health concerns about teen drinking and how the horrors of drunk driving had become too real. At least part of the controversy surrounding the episode was the result of the activism of Mothers Against Drunk Driving in the late 1970s and early 1980s—which leads to the next lesson, "Friends Don't Let Friends Drink and Drive."

Lesson Three
"Friends Don't Let Friends Drink and Drive"

I made the creature a botanist vegetarian who never eats meat, only junk food, vegetables, and Coors.

— STEVEN SPIELBERG[1]

Released in 1982, *E.T. the Extra-Terrestrial* earned approximately $13 million in its first three days, broke box office records, and remains one of the highest-grossing films in North America.[2] *E.T.* is "not merely the film itself and what it signifies, but the commercial hype, the American critics' reviews, the public response, the T-shirts, the children's games, the candy advertisements. It represents a moment in American cultural history," and a mythic white suburban U.S. childhood.[3] At the world premiere of *E.T.*, Spielberg stated that he "wanted to become a child to make this movie," shooting the scenes from a child's eye view. In answer to a question about *E.T.*'s popularity, a psychiatrist suggested that the screenplay tapped into the "timeless appeal of childhood innocence."[4] Borrowing from classic children's literature, especially *The Wonderful Wizard of Oz* and *Peter Pan*, screenwriter Melissa Mathison entwines coming-of-age with nostalgia.[5] Writing in *The New York Times*, film critic Vincent Canby notes that "E.T. is as contemporary as laser beam technology, but it's full of the timeless longings expressed in children's literature of all eras."[6] Canby and other critics rightly point out that the script follows a familiar narrative in which the child underdog overcomes obstacles through pluck, hope, and a little magic.

Yet, this feel-good tale of childhood innocence is at heart a sci-fi horror movie in which an alien temporarily uses a 10-year-old boy as its host and through psychokinesis gets the unknowing child drunk. The drinking scene begins roughly forty-five minutes into the film when the alien, left home alone, looks for something to eat in the fridge. After spitting out a mouthful of potato salad, it discovers and guzzles down at least a six-pack of Coors Banquet beer. E.T. and Elliott share a telekinetic link and as the alien gets increasingly intoxicated, so does the boy. The camera crosscuts between E.T. at the house and Elliott sitting at a desk in a classroom where his teacher instructs the children on how to use sharp scalpels to dissect a chloroformed frog in their human anatomy unit. The instructor assures the class that the animals will feel no pain even as he instructs them to observe the intestines going through peristaltic action and to locate the amphibian's beating heart once their frog is cut open. As Elliott listens, E.T. pounds his first beer in the kitchen and the boy burps out loud causing mixed responses of laughter and groans of disgust from classmates. When E.T. bumps his head, Elliott feels it; and when the alien falls on the kitchen floor, Elliott slides out of his desk. John Williams' score adds to the light-heartedness of the scene. As Elliott's tipsiness increases and E.T. communicates his desire to be set free and go home, Elliott finds the courage to release the frogs. He frees the doomed animals and, in an evocation of horror conventions in films like the 1972 *Frogs*, the amphibians cover the classroom floor, terrifying the other children.

When Elliott tries on drunkenness, he becomes a pint-size John Wayne, tapping into a tough guy persona and familiar associations between heteromasculinity and intoxication embedded in the drinking curriculum.[7] When E.T. turns the television channel to a scene from John Ford's *The Quiet Man*, he sees the hero grab, restrain, and kiss Maureen O'Hara. The camera then shifts to Elliott mimicking Wayne's behavior as the tipsy boy grips the girl in his class (played by future Playboy Playmate, Erika Eleniak), and stands on the back of another student to kiss her on the lips without her consent. Elliott's rebellion gets him hauled away to the principal's office. While drunkenness fuels Elliott's confidence, intoxication boosts E.T.'s creativity as the alien makes ingenious ties between a Buck Rogers comic strip and a telephone commercial. The alien invents a way to "phone home" while blitzed, exemplifying Edward Slingerland's thesis that "getting drunk, high, or otherwise cognitively altered must have, over evolutionary time, helped individuals to survive and flourish, and cultures to endure and expand."[8]

E.T. is not an outlier in the representation of drinking and intoxication in children's texts. Like the Cowardly Lion in L. Frank Baum's 1900 *The Wonderful Wizard of Oz* and Dumbo in the Walt Disney film, Elliott receives a dose of "liquid courage" from an outside source.[9] This is no surprise as performances of drunkenness are "associated with desirable outcomes and characteristics" in family films from Disney to DreamWorks.[10] Elliott's tipsi-ness is unremarkable. Reviewers of the film in 1982 either ignore or comment favorably on the drunken child scene. A critic for *The Christian Science Monitor* overlooks the buzzed school-aged child, focusing on other elements, like profanity, that they find inappropriate, writing that it "would be an ideal family film if not for a few vulgar words, and a sci-fi medical sequence preceding the 'Peter Pan' style climax."[11] At least two reviewers find the scene funny, commenting that Elliott "hilariously instructs the alien in the modes of modern American life: he is introduced to Star Wars toys, makes the acquaintance of cartoon shows and gets really chummy with a six-pack of Coors."[12] A writer for *Newsweek* similarly notes that E.T. and Elliott go on a symbiotic voyage that results in a "hilarious crescendo" after Elliott gets "soused on beer."[13]

About E.T., Canby asks, "What are the lessons he has to teach Elliott, who comes to identify with E.T. so closely that when E.T. is left alone in the house, goes on a beer binge, it's Elliott, several miles away in school, who burps and becomes serenely smashed?"[14] Indeed, what lessons is E.T. teaching Elliott and the audience through this scene of telekinetic drunkenness? In partial answer to this question, *E.T.* the film, its circulation, and the decade of the 1980s instructs about the co-expression of horror and humor. Reviewers read the scene as funny because of the incongruity of the child acting like an adult, and the comedic physicality of drunkenness baked into cultural representations of intoxication, like those in the animated shorts discussed in the last lesson, which evoke laughter via slapstick comedy.

Violence—from alien possession to a classroom of scalpel-wielding children—informs the scene of inebriation. Indeed, *E.T.* was originally intended to be a horror film entitled *Night Skies* in which aliens terrorize a middle-class family by touching them with a long bony finger. Spielberg made *E.T.* into a more hopeful story and saved the scaring of a suburban family for *Poltergeist* (in that 1982 movie, the young Carol Anne Freeling is also taken over by a supernatural being). In *E.T.*, the middle-class suburb is charmed rather than harmed by the stranger. These two approaches to a story of alien invasion aligned as pleasure and fear draw close together when children are in the spotlight.

Elliott's intoxication is involuntary; his drunkenness doesn't lessen his innocence but rather intensifies it. He's pranked by the stranger in his house for the audience's delight. The comedy of E.T.'s drunkenness, like Elliott's, is based on innocence. Neither understands what is happening. Laughter can be a form of aggression as it is in this scene; the pleasure of this potentially dangerous binge drinking rests in the physical vulnerability and naiveté that makes these two characters Other to adults. Both are confined to spaces associated with children—the home and the school—and ultimately no harm is done, which allows the audience to relish in comedic violence. It is only when "something veers from harmless incongruity into potentially dangerous territory" that the line between humor and horror is made visible.[15] If, for instance, Elliott was a teenager his drinking would be more expected and less incongruous, or if E.T. drank beer and then got behind the wheel of a car, as the teens in the graphic public service announcements discussed here later do, then the scene would no longer be played for laughs. In E.T., like other texts in the drinking curriculum, childishness and intoxication are mutually dependent, reiterating associations of childhood with Otherness—Elliott and E.T. (the child and his pet) are not proper adult subjects.[16]

E.T. reflects the economic and social worries of the conservative Reagan years, which included growing class divisions, as well as anxieties about youth. Neil Postman decried the "disappearance of childhood" in the 1980s, and E.T. engages with concerns including, "rising divorce rates, the questioning of authority, the women's movement (which some believed contributed to the breakdown of traditional family structures), as well as the sexual revolution itself . . ."[17] Indeed, E.T. infiltrates the home because Elliott's father has left his wife and family. More importantly, as Elliott burps and loses control of his body and E.T. totters around the suburban home, both expose and tamp down fears about out-of-control children and Others. Concerns about the breakdown of the white nuclear family are played out through the innocent child made vulnerable by an outside influence. This threat is ultimately shored up because of Elliott's status as a privileged white suburban child. The audience watches in horror and then laughs with relief that the white child is not harmed by the outsider in his midst.

However, given public health concerns about alcoholism in general and teenage drinking in particular during this decade (as well as Nancy Reagan's widely publicized youth drug education campaign "Just Say No") the lack of concern over Elliott's drinking may at first seem confounding. Yet what seems like a contradiction is the very essence of the drinking curriculum—the lessons about the pleasures of alcohol consumption co-exist with exhortations about its dangers. Even as concerns about alcohol in this decade ultimately coalesced around teenage drinking and resulted in a cultural reckoning with drunk driving through the activism of Mothers Against Drunk Driving, E.T.'s lessons in the pleasures of childhood inebriation did not waver during this conservative crack-down on youth and alcohol.

"That Girl Was My Daughter"

At a 1980 traffic safety conference, Candy Lightner delivered a speech about a 13-year-old girl who had been killed by a serial drunk driver with several previous convictions. At the end of her talk, she told the audience: "That girl was my daughter." Lightner's anger and grief-ridden speech ignited one of the most important social movements in the history of alcohol in the United States.[18] Lightner went on to form the grassroots organization Mothers Against Drunk Drivers, which later changed its name to Mothers Against Drunk Driving. The group was born out of the horror stories of Lightner's children. Her 18-month-old daughter Serena was injured when a drunken driver rear-ended their car; Lightner's son Travis was run over six years later by an impaired driver and in addition to broken bones suffered permanent brain damage (the driver had no license and received no ticket). Clarence William Busch, out on bail for previous hit and runs while drunk, killed Lightner's daughter, Cari, on her way to a church carnival. Cari was his fifth offense in four years. Lightner started MADD the day after her daughter's funeral on May 7, 1980. Busch spent only nine months in jail after pleading no contest to vehicular manslaughter.[19] Busch's short jail time is evidence of how before the activism on behalf of victims by MADD, drunk driving crashes were considered "accidents" and there was little accountability for the predominately white male offenders aged 21–44.[20]

The federal government had previously made efforts to bring awareness to the dangers of drinking and driving, including the 1970 National Safety Council's "Scream Bloody Murder" newspaper, magazine, radio, and television campaign. The NSC's televised PSA repackaged the innocent young child murdered by a habitual drunkard from temperance fiction discussed in the first lesson of this book. The voice-over claims that the drunk driver "stops overcrowding the classroom"; the camera captures a group of young children and then pans to one empty desk. While the NSC used elementary schoolchildren as victims, teenagers were the culprits in the U.S. Department of Transportation/National Highway Traffic Safety Administration's 1976 pamphlet *How to Talk to Your Teenager About Drinking and Driving*.[21] MADD, too, would put the spotlight on teenagers and in so doing enter an ongoing debate about legal minimum age drinking laws in the United States.

After Prohibition's repeal in 1933, the legal drinking age in most states was set at 21.[22] This was mostly settled until 1971 when the legal voting age dropped to 18 as a result of the "social upheaval of the 1960s and the Vietnam War draft lottery."[23] After this point, "nearly half the states dropped the drinking age to

18, 19, and 20."[24] This change raised concerns as research suggested a strong correlation between an increase in traffic fatalities among youth and the lowered minimum legal drinking age, which resulted in some states reversing their decision. Thus, both anxieties about teens' overuse of alcohol and the related issue of drinking and driving took center stage in the 1980s. Countless headlines in mainstream publications like *Good Housekeeping* sounded the alarm with titles like "Is *Your* Child a Secret Alcoholic?"[25] A 1982 *New York Times* article defined "a flood of teen-age drinking that increasingly alarms parents, educators, the police, doctors and government officials—in fact, all of society" and suggested the possibility of teaching youth in school how to drink alcohol safely.[26]

By 1988 alcohol was heralded in *The New York Times* as "The Teen Drug of Choice."[27] The popular girls' magazine *Seventeen* ran a special corporately sponsored supplement "When will teens sober up? They drink, they drive, and they die."[28] The controversial piece used yearbook pictures of teens murdered by drunk drivers and noted that because adolescents were new to both drinking and driving that this made them the most vulnerable to being maimed or killed. The authors pulled on horror and statistics to grab readers' attention.

> The numbers alone can give you the shivers: Roughly 9,000 teenagers die each year in motor-vehicle accidents. If you have a hard time picturing 9,000 kids all at once, imagine one average-size math class vanishing from the face of the earth every day for a year. Of those 9,000 teens who die, <u>over half</u> are slaughtered in crashes caused by drunkenness at the wheel. While teenagers number only 8 percent of the total driver population in the United States, they make up 15 percent of the causalities in alcohol-related accidents.[29]

The black-and-white illustration that accompanies the article pictures an arm in a letterman sweater hanging out of the car and a beer can on the ground, creating a new iconography of drunk driving that implicated the teen as both victim and perpetrator (see Figure 22).

MADD's activism, like other crescendos in the history of alcohol in the United States, used youth as lightning rods for change. Specifically, MADD focused its efforts on educating teenagers and on raising the national minimum age back to 21. MADD's political reach was impressive. Reagan appointed Lightner to the national commission on drunk driving in 1982. On July 17, 1984, he signed the National Minimum Drinking Age Act that withheld federal highway funds from U.S. states that failed to set the legal drinking age at 21.

WHEN WILL TEENS SOBER UP?

They Drink, They Drive —and They Die

The numbers alone can give you the shivers: Roughly 9,000 teenagers die each year in motor-vehicle accidents. If you have a hard time picturing 9,000 kids all at once, imagine one average-size math class vanishing from the face of the earth every day for a year. Of those 9,000 teens who die, <u>over half</u> are slaughtered in crashes caused by drunkenness at the wheel. While teenagers number only 8 percent of the total driver population in the United States, they make up 15 percent of the casualties in alcohol-related accidents. Over the past two decades, as life expectancy in this country has improved for every other age group, the *(continued on next page)*

Figure 22. *Seventeen*, November 1983

By 1988 all states had adopted 21 as the legal drinking age. MADD also lobbied to lower the legal blood alcohol level to .08.

PSAs in the 1980s aimed to curtail teen drunk driving by advocating abstinence and preventing "alcohol-related problems before they begin."[30] Drawing on the visceral scare tactics of horror films, PSAs put a contemporary spin on the legacies of graphic violence that dominated nineteenth-century temperance texts for the child and that visualized the horrific demise of youth at the hands of drunken adults (see Figure 23). The drunkard was now a teenage boy the same age as his victims. The U.S. Ad Council and the U.S. Department of Transportation's 1983 "Skeletons," a thirty-second PSA is exemplary. In the video, Michael Jackson's "Beat It" from the album *Thriller* plays in the background as a group of white teens get into a car with a drunk male adolescent driver in a letterman jacket.[31] As the music plays, a voice-over says: "If you don't stop your friend from drinking and driving, you're as good as dead. Drinking and driving can kill a friendship." The four healthy, vibrant, and tipsy teens in the car transform into skeletons as soon as the key turns in the ignition.

MADD ushered in a shift in the drinking curriculum from a focus on adult drunk drivers to drunk driving and adolescents, redrawing the fuzzy lines between adulthood and childhood. Targeting teens was an easy way for politicians to avoid creating structures that might curtail the power of the alcohol industry. MADD's crusade packaged anxieties about alcoholism, youth, and drunk driving into a cause. MADD's activism resulted in new laws, tougher sentences, money for enforcement, victim support, and education for teens about the dangers of driving under the influence. That teenagers became the face of drunk driving education and reform is evident in the final 1983 *Commission Report*, which concludes that "in order to reduce the death rate of American youth, the minimum legal drinking age for all alcoholic beverages should be raised to 21."[32]

To be sure, the pathologizing of teenagers fit into a long-standing fear of and anxiety about childhood, but it also cemented the adolescent as a distinct category. Some critics argued that the Drinking Age Act infringed on the rights of youth. In 1985 in an article for *The Nation* titled "The New Anti-Youth Movement" Ted Galen Carpenter argued that "the drinking-age bill is a hoax, a cynical attempt to use young adults as scapegoats for a complex national problem" and that the drinking bill is just one episode "in a campaign to restrict the rights of adults under 21 years of age and adolescents—a counterrevolution, in effect, which threatens important gains young people made during the late 1960s and the 1970s."[33] Drinking age legislation, then, is also about defining the limits of childhood and youth agency. As Carpenter suggests, the National

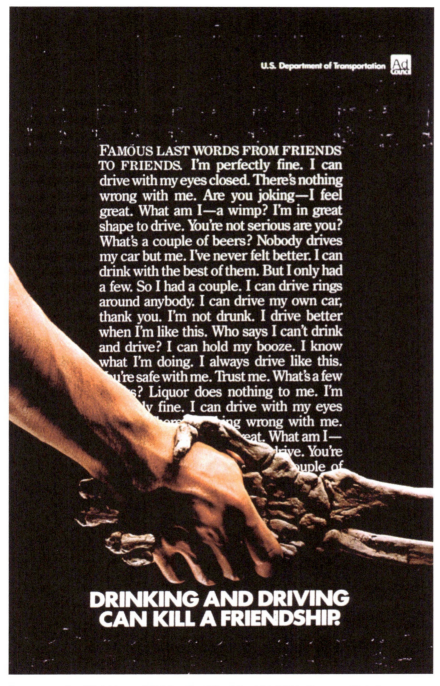

Figure 23. 1980s "Drinking and Driving Can Kill a Friendship" PSA. Courtesy, Digital Collections—National Library of Medicine.

Minimum Drinking Age Act, while cloaked in the discourse of protection, reveals a "hostility toward the legal rights of minors."[34] Furthermore, this legislation occurred during a period of social conservatism in which other constraints that had disappeared in the 1960s, like dress codes and curfew laws, were re-emerging. Like the drinking age requirement, these laws were also about taking away rights for youth's own good and for securing white middle-class norms of respectability. Similarly, Joseph R. Gusfield in his history of the construction of alcohol problems notes that "since the 1960s, America has witnessed the rise of a new 'dangerous class' whose relation to social structure is less determined by the division of labor than by the division of age. The invention of adolescence as a distinct social category in the twentieth century has provided a new image of the criminal class and a new source of threat and fear."[35] The result is a form of age segregation; the United States remains "one of only a handful of nations in the world with a minimum drinking age of 21."[36]

Circling back to *E.T.*, Elliott's humorous drunken antics seem out of place during a social panic about youth and drinking. Yet, the child's innocence sets up the teenager's depravity. Categories of child and teenager are culturally constructed in part through alcohol and its associations with misbehavior. The young child can be humorously intoxicated because they remain vulnerable while adolescent alcohol consumption is associated with dangers such as teenage pregnancy, vandalism, violence, and traffic fatalities. The coexistence of the horrors of drunk driving and the humor of the tipsy Elliott during this cultural moment are two sides of the same coin: intoxication sanctions the depiction of violence against youth through both fear and laughter. This sentiment squares with the pretense of the drinking curriculum, which claims to protect youth from the dangers of drunkenness while at the same time condoning the pleasures of alcohol.

E.T. Walks Into a Bar

Though there is no drunk driving in *E.T.*, the film nonetheless folds into the cultural reckoning with it that MADD ushered in. Most discussions about branding in the film center around Reese's Pieces and how the sales of the candy skyrocketed after the film.[37] Less discussed are the other commodities in the movie, including Coke, Pez, and most importantly for this discussion, Coors Banquet beer. Like Mars, Inc., which turned down the opportunity to have M&M's in the film, Anheuser-Busch declined the invitation to have their product featured in *E.T.* "because beer was used for the questionable purpose of intoxicating a child, not to mention an extraterrestrial."[38] Coors, however, said yes, perhaps in part to remedy the brand's dip in popularity and its reputation as the AFL-CIO called for its member unions to boycott the company in 1977, the same year the beer was featured in the film *Smokey and the Bandit*, to support striking workers experiencing inequities at the company's Golden, Colorado–based brewery.[39] Additionally, Coors was popular with youth, leading one reporter to comment that "compared with Heineken or other more full-bodied foreign beers, Coors does seem almost flavorless, and it is this quality that could account for its popularity among young people just starting to get acquainted with the pleasures of beer drinking."[40] Overall, the marketing of Coors within and outside the film to and through young people gives an added dimension to the "Friends Don't Let Friends Drink and Drive" lesson.

In a 1982 bar poster created for an anti-drinking and driving campaign, E.T. stands behind the counter with an apron on and his signature glowing finger up in the air (see Figure 24). The message reads: "If you go beyond your limit, please don't drive. 'Phone Home.'" The PSA demonstrates how MADD might have changed the cultural conversation about drinking and driving in the 1980s, but the liquor industry continued to actively promote its products at sporting events and bars to which people drove. Barron H. Lerner notes that prior to World War II, most public imbibing happened in cities where people had access to easy transportation; suburban growth in the 1950s, home ownership, and white flight from urban centers normalized drinking and driving.[41] Addressing public concerns about drunk driving, companies pivoted to voluntary responsibility campaigns that served as an outward sign of goodwill and that moved discussions away from any changes in policy or law about where and how a corporation could sell alcohol.

These responsibility messages fit with the conservative ethos of the 1980s. Whereas the nineteenth-century temperance movement and the anti-saloon league sought to ban the sale and consumption of alcohol in public spaces, the social conservativism of the 1980s focused on individual responsibility.[42] This ideology is exemplified by a 1981 special-edition stamp from the U.S. Postal Service that proclaimed: "Alcoholism, you can beat it!" The "you" in the statement suggests individuals could overcome alcoholism if they got treatment. Addiction is a battle, like the "war on drugs," to be won.

Coors, then, framed their PSA "within the problem of drunk driving, which implies that drinking excessively can still be done responsibly as long as no driving is involved."[43] Responsible drinking campaigns rely on mixed lessons—a warning about potential dangers and "images of drinking as a social lubricant, form of release or escape, or way to gain social status."[44] In this way, E.T. both instructs us to be responsible and reminds us of the delights of intoxication.

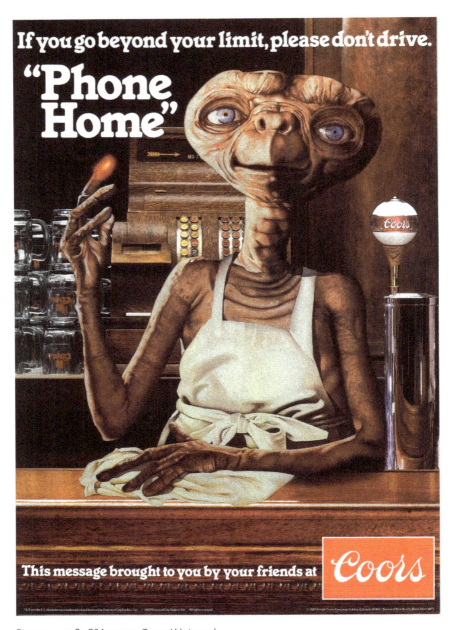

Figure 24. 1983 PSA poster. Coors / Universal.

Coors temperance washes its brand through family entertainment as it nods to the humorous scene in which the alien and Elliott get telekinetically tipsy. If a six-pack of Banquet beer cannot harm them, it certainly won't be dangerous to an adult, which in 1982 included 19-year-olds legally able to purchase and drink Coors in bars in some states west of the Mississippi, including Idaho and Arizona.

The relationship between *E.T.* and Coors demonstrates how the liquor industry and the children's culture industry are intimately entwined rather than the separate spheres we might wish them to be. The *E.T.* PSA is a flashpoint in the drinking curriculum that captures the rising assertion of individual responsibility as the correct antidote to controlling alcohol consumption and addiction. The "Friends Don't Let Friends Drink and Drive" lesson, though, teaches us more than just moral responsibility. It instructs us that throughout the 1980s, it is through the teenager that anxieties about alcohol are filtered, and it is through intoxication that fears of the childlike are managed.

E.T. remains a classic children's film and a nostalgic touchpoint. In 2017, the Pop Classics series, a division of Penguin Random House that publishes adaptations of iconic films and television shows from the 1980s, made the script into a picture book. Marketed for a young audience, the style is cartoony and bright. Pop Classics describes its products in the following way.

> The films and TV shows that families love are reimagined as lively, colorful picture books featuring the iconic moments and characters of the original. Simple words are paired with a kid-friendly storybook format that's perfect for bedtime or story time. All-new illustrations done in classic picture book style make this series a great way for parents to share their pop culture favorites with a new generation.

In *E.T. the Extra-Terrestrial: The Classic Illustrated Storybook* the references to beer are airbrushed out. Following William Kotzwinkle's 1982 novelization, *E.T. the Extra-Terrestrial in His Adventure on Earth*, the drunken classroom scene is also omitted. In the Pop Classics storybook, illustrator Kim Smith draws the scene in the kitchen and includes the alien spitting out potato salad; however, Coors Banquet beer is absent.[45] The editing out of the beer-drinking scene to make the book "kid-friendly" may seem common sense, however, it doesn't make the alcohol magically go away. Ultimately, the question of whether intoxication or alcohol is appropriate children's fare is window dressing that hides the uncomfortable fact that alcohol is etched into children's culture. What *E.T.* the film suggests is that the drinking curriculum requires cognitive dissonance—its lessons are built on pleasure, which walks a fine line between laughter and fear. In addition, while we focus on the appropriateness of materials for youth, we miss how images and stories of drunkenness index our conflicting feelings about children. After all, the "timeless appeal of childhood innocence" that the film evokes relies on a drunken school-aged boy as a punchline in the script, revealing a soft antagonism toward youth. *E.T.* leaves us with an unsettling question, when did the drinking child become funny? That is the subject of the next lesson.

Lesson Four

It's Funny When Kids Drink

"Humor depends on the neighborhood it's born in."

— WILLIAM ELDER

Drinking or soon-to-be-drunk children are the punch line of William Elder's spoof advertisement, "Visiting the Grandparents," published in the April 1956 issue of *MAD Magazine* (see Figure 25). The image advocates boozing together as a family affair: a baby downs a glass of beer while a doting mother dangles a can opener above the bassinet, a grandmother gives the infant a tiny doll (definitely not approved for children under three) that holds a pint-size glass of beer in their plastic hand, and a school age girl grasping a drink snuggles up against the older woman.[1] A cheerful red-headed boy (who bears a striking resemblance to the magazine's fictitious cover boy Alfred E. Neuman) sits on his grandfather's lap bonding over a cold one. The father, who occupies the center top of the panel and positioned visually as head of the household, cheerfully misses his glass, pouring his beer onto the floor. The picture bursts with what *MAD* founder Harvey Kurtzman called Elder's "hilarious clutter," which Elder defined as "Chicken Fat"—"the extra little non-sequitur gags that he crammed into his panels." The parrot and the family dog drink beer, a bouquet of flowers sits in alcohol, and the platter displayed behind the grandfather suggests the phrase "drinks like a fish" which the animal in the bowl literally does, bubbles foaming out the top of the bowl. Satirizing protectionist discourses in which children are in danger when alcohol is present, Elder draws intemperate children who are safe and sound. Everyone and everything in the picture is happily headed down the road to drunkenness without any threat of violence.

"VISITING THE GRANDPARENTS" by William Elder. *Number 1 in the series "Ol' Home Life."*

While you are visiting—

What makes a glass of beer taste so good?

Malted barley—with important body minerals plus liquid matter. For thing that makes glass of beer taste so good is terrible thirst.

Tangy hops. Yes—visiting can be a series of tangy hops if you play your cards right. And you'd be surprised how good free beer tastes!

The way it "goes with everything"—makes beer this country's Beverage of Moderation—the way it fits into our friendly way of life—the way each glass makes us friendlier and friendlier and friendlier.

Beer Belongs—Enjoy It!

Figure 25. William Elder, "Visiting the Grandparents," *MAD*, April 1956.

The humor of the image rests on the knowledge that "Visiting the Grand-parents" is a parody of the "Beer Belongs" advertising campaign, one of the most successful and longest-running alcohol marketing drives in the U.S., pro-duced by the United States Brewers Foundation between 1945 and 1956. To fully understand Elder's joke, it is important to understand that the Brewers Foundation actively sought to shift the location of drinking from the public to the private as a strategy to retool beer's association with seedy taverns, poverty, immigrants, and the working class. To proactively avert a return to the prohi-bition of alcohol, the Brewers Foundation launched a visual series of numbered prints drawn by famous American artists in a range of styles that pictured pros-perous white upper-middle-class adults playing croquet and tennis while drinking a glass of beer or seated next to bottles of it.[2] Elder mocks this limited-edition element, noting at the bottom of the ad that his image is the first in the "Ol' Home Life" series.

The campaign's depiction of American home life and belonging was nar-row. The print advertisements included the following message: "For beer and ale are the kind of beverages Americans like. They belong—to pleasant living, to good fellowship, to sensible moderation. And our right to enjoy them, this too belongs—to our own American heritage of personal freedom." This belong-ing is framed by absence. No people of color are represented. Likewise, Elder, a Jewish artist, would not have found himself reflected in the "America" in the ads.[3] Elder changes the Brewers' campaign tagline from "America's Beverage of Moderation" to "The Beverage of Moderation Foundation to Encourage Excess." Excess speaks to the intemperance of the adults and the relegation of children, as a surplus that cannot and should not be seen. Indeed, children are conspicuously absent in the "Home Life in America" series, even in scenes in which you'd expect to see them, like holiday gatherings. In Douglass Crock-well's 1949 "Thanksgiving" and "Decorating for Christmas," for instance, only adults are visible. Elder critiques this absence and its disavowal of the child's potential intemperance by inserting children into his spoof.

The melding of alcohol, childhood, and pleasure in the same scene, then, creates a provocative spectacle. The inclusion of the child in Elder's parody makes it a successful gag because of the juxtaposition of cute white upper-middle-class children with carefree and joyful alcohol consumption. Elder's image reminds us that childhood has not always been associated with sobriety and that alcohol holds the potential to make adults act childish or childlike. "Visiting the Grandparents" satirizes the visual hypocrisy of an advertising campaign that pays lip service to moderation but markets itself through images of white upper-middle class adults drinking *all* the time without trou-ble. "Visiting the Grandparents" provides an entry point for considering the politics of drinking child humor within the context and tradition of U.S. comics.

As Elder's spoof ad suggests, drinking child humor connects skepticism about and a willingness to skewer the corporate innocence industry to which images of children are central. Before "Visiting the Grandparents," Elder had already made a career out of disrupting cute images of white youth in his work for *MAD*.[4] Along with Kurtzman, Elder drew *Starchie!* (*MAD* #12 1954) a parody of the "Archie" comics in which the clean-cut all-American Archie and Jughead are represented as cigarette-smoking juvenile delinquents. They also created "Mickey Rodent" (*MAD* #19 1955), presented by "Walt Dizzy," which incorporated Yiddish, and, among other gags, pictured Mickey as an unshaven character with a mousetrap on his finger and a small naked child on a leash held by one of the animals.

MAD was a publication geared to and primarily read by youth. Even Alfred E. Neuman, the mascot for the publication, was a child.[5] By the time Elder's "Visiting the Grandparents" was published, *MAD* "was second in popularity among high school students to *Life* magazine."[6] Elder and other cartoonists for *MAD* assumed that their young audience were sophisticated cultural critics. Through parodies of corporate culture, *MAD* comics artists altered both images of childhood as well as ideas about the young reader's supposed vulnerability as youth were already in on the joke.

Perhaps most importantly, *MAD* cartoonists jammed the machine that corporate culture used to manufacture childhood innocence, scrambling its messages and its myths, including the child's relationship to and with alcohol.[7] This work resonated with and influenced numerous other cartoonists, including Art Spiegelman and Lynda Barry. Spiegelman has stated that he "studied *MAD* the way some kids studied the Talmud."[8] Elder and Kurtzman, among other cartoonists at *MAD*, cleared the way for unique satirical and boundary-breaking projects in which alcohol and childhood merged for comic effect within a particular moment in the United States. One of the most critical examples of this influence is the *Wacky Packages* bubble gum trading cards produced by the Topps Corporation in the late 1960s, which reached their height of popularity from 1973 to 1975.

Wacky Packages: Drinking Fun in the Childhood Underground

Wacky Packages bubble gum trading cards are a pop culture phenomenon first released in 1967 and developed by a creative team of underground comix artists, most notably Art Spiegelman and Jay Lynch, for the Topps Corporation.[9] In 1973 the cards were released as peel-and-stick stickers, at which point a reporter claimed that *Wacky Packages* were "the hottest thing since Hula

Hoops."[10] The stickers were tiny, measuring just two by three inches, and the children that collected and traded them made them popular. *Wacky Packages* came with one piece of bubble gum, two stickers, and a puzzle piece printed on the back for a larger Wacky poster. The gum was of secondary importance. One commentator opined: "The one thing no kid seems to buy *Wacky Packages* for is the gum—this may be the only product in the loony history of American capitalism that gets thrown away *before* the wrapper." Reflecting in 2002 on the making of *Wacky Packages* and their cultural import, Jay Lynch states:

> I think we all regarded what we were doing as just a way to make a living at the time. Wacky Packages . . . Funny Little Joke Books . . . Bazooka Joe. . . . cards of funny monsters . . . We never gave any of this all that much thought. But now, thirty-some-odd years later, Wacky Packages have become some sort of historical icons.[11]

Wacky Packages' popularity stemmed from spoofs of familiar brands and thus shared an affinity with parodies like Elder's that were published in *MAD*. Indeed, Spiegelman wrote that *Wacky Packages* were "an obvious platform for feeding my *MAD* lessons back to another generation," and that the trading cards formed "a young child's first exposure to subverting adult consumer culture."[12] As such, the cards delivered mini-lessons in rebellion for youth aged six to fourteen. Spiegelman writes that the stickers were created "much like the way early comic books were made: They certainly weren't made as art, they weren't sold as art, and they weren't thought of as art. Wacky Packages just formed an island of subversive underground culture in the surrounding sea of junk."[13] The diminutive form and childish humor of the *Wacky Packages* cards articulated deep suspicion about cuteness, childhood, and innocence.

Wacky Packages unsettled familiar images and stories of childhood innocence that hinged on temperance for meaning. The stickers challenged adult authority as they advertised child-unfriendly products and soaked child-friendly ones in alcohol. Mock liquor advertisements were a common *Wacky Packages* gag as was the picturing of drunks. Exemplary stickers include: "Moonshine Wheez-It—Whiskey Flavored Crackers: Eat Yourself Drunk!" and "Plastered Whiskey Flavored Peanuts: Favored by drinkers everywhere." Other *Wacky Packages* jokes encouraged children to get adults drunk: "Give Old Grand-Mom this whiskey and watch her fall off her rocking chair" and overhauled child-friendly products for drunkenness, such as the "200 Proof Tipsy Roll Pop for Real Suckers: You'll Roll in the Street Pop!" Artists assumed that youth would understand the gags which required young people's exposure to the products through corporate marketing or through first-hand knowledge. Thus, drunk children were also fair game for *Wacky Packages* spoofs, such as ads like

"Get Drunk With Alcohol Seltzer" that mocked the pixie Speedy Alka-Seltzer, the small, cute, baby-faced character used to sell the effervescent tablets from 1951 to 1980 as a falling down, hiccupping drunk.[14] In 1973, the Topps Company published *Brandy Land Game,* one of their funniest and gag-filled drinking child stickers.

The *Brandy Land* sticker parodies one of the most saccharine of all children's board games, *Candy Land,* and a brief overview of the game adds to an understanding of the spoof. Milton Bradley released *Candy Land* in 1949. Schoolteacher Eleanor Abbott invented the game for children recovering in polio wards during the epidemic of the 1940s and 1950s.[15] Originally intended for young children spending time in an iron lung, the game requires no strategy. *Candy Land* embodies the cute aesthetic governing visual images of normative white childhood since the latter part of the nineteenth century, which makes it a perfect target for satire.[16] On the game box lid, the small children's round arms and button noses invite the viewer to pinch their cheeks and delight at the prospect of a trip to the fantastical nonthreatening Candy Land. The visual imagery and concept of the game provide a stark contrast to more familiar tales of hungry children abandoned in the woods who starve to death like the "The Babes in the Woods" or who encounter a child-eating witch in a candy house like Hansel and Gretel. *Candy Land* boasts a sterilized landscape of innocence in which only good things happen, marketing a romanticized vision of cute and cuddly well-behaved children to adult consumers.

Of course, cute is a racialized concept in the United States that works in tandem with how innocence became the province of white childhood in the latter half of the nineteenth century when Black children "were increasingly and overwhelmingly evacuated of innocence."[17] The *Candy Land* children are associated with "symbolic properties and qualities that define the cute in a white supremacist culture (white skin, blond hair, blue eyes); and the culturally specific ways in which consumers or spectators learn to 'recognize' and 'value' the cute."[18] *Candy Land* is advertised as "a sweet little game for sweet little folks," and in the hands of the *Wacky Packages* artists the sweet little game for sweet little folks turns sour (see Figure 26).

Wacky Packages cartoonists use subversive humor to link white childhood to addiction and excess rather than purity and sweetness. Monstrosity replaces cuteness as the petite facial features of the original children are exaggerated to include swollen red noses and badly cut hair. The girl's dress is now ill-fitting and somehow so short that it flies up in the back; she has lost her shoe, revealing a toe that pops out of an un-mended sock. Stripped of cuteness, the Brandy Land children are detached from vulnerability, and as the visuality tilts more

Figure 26. *Brandy Land Wacky Packages* Sticker, 1973.

toward depravity, the viewer is less sympathetic to their plight. Part of the reason these tippling tots do not motivate sentimentality in the viewer lies with the visual coding of poverty. Viewers are guided to laugh out loud at the absurdity of the image, drinking children in a disreputable state are made more adultlike.

Thus, the *Brandy Land* children do not solicit adult protection or empathy even though they are drinking alcohol. The sticker is full of visual gags about liquor, of what Spiegelman called "*MAD* density."[19] The saccharine landscape of donuts, cupcakes, and candy canes, is redrawn as a carnivalesque scene of beer and booze bottles, including a large bottle marked with XXX, and the requisite pink elephant game piece. *Brandy Land* eschews educational and parental gatekeepers. The game is approved by Boozers and Losers!!!, a martini glass and the phrase "Get Drunk Playing This" stands in for the Milton Bradley "Key to Fun" logo. No longer limited to ages 4–8, the *Brandy Land* game is intended "For Drunks of all Ages" and is "One Hundred Proof." These gags call attention to both the social construction of drunkenness as an adult behavior and the childish attributes that alcohol advertisements often reference like play, wide open natural spaces, and leisure. Artists at Topps expanded the drinking curriculum, offering their child audience a subversive perspective on corporate marketing of drinking culture and at the same time echoed cautionary graphic lessons about the harm of intemperance.

To be sure, *Wacky Packages* artists broke ground when they pictured drinking children as funny, bringing back into the visual field possibilities that had been stifled through a host of cultural mechanisms, including the nineteenth-century temperance movement's deployment of the sober child to mark innocence and morality. Perhaps even more powerfully, *Wacky Packages* parodies critiqued the marketing of alcohol, pinpointing how the broader drinking curriculum in the United States both tempts children to drink and disavows any such encouragement. The jokes were aimed specifically at a child audience who the creators knew were already critically literate enough to get the graphically coded humor. *Wacky Packages* creators constructed the child consumer as an astute cultural critic, a youngster adept at discerning parody, who could look at funny pictures of drinking children without heading to the fridge for a beer.

On the other hand, *Wacky Packages*, pop culture objects from the children's underground, might also be read as temperance lessons delivered in subversive packaging, a spoonful of humor with a dose of reality about the harmful effects of drinking. *Wacky Packages*, like Elder's "Visiting the Grandparents," discourage drinking through exaggerations and stereotypes.[20] The young drunkards in *Brandy Land* evoke feelings of disgust and laughter rather than pity or affection as they walk down a boozy gumdrop lane. The creative team at *Wacky Packages* disrupted idyllic representations of white middle-class childhood by drawing on a long-standing visual archive discussed in the "D is for Drunkard" lesson.

The Topps company extended their work throughout the 1980s to offer up more grotesque representations of children with the *Garbage Pail Kids* sticker series that included the character Boozin' Bruce / Drunk Ken, a tottering figure hanging onto a lamppost about to fall into a manhole while drooling and holding a baby bottle full of "ol rot gut," surrounded by a pink elephant, a blue rabbit, and a green snake.[21] Through *Wacky Packages*, *Garbage Pail Kids*, and other comic outlets, childhood drinking humor both discouraged intoxication and documented its possible pleasures.

Lynda Barry's Funny / Not Funny Drunk Girls

In *Picture This*, one of Lynda Barry's cartoon girls, Arna, peeks at the cover of the book and asks, "Was it a book for kids or grown-ups? The monkey drank beer, played cards, and bought lottery tickets. Was that a good influence?" (see Figure 27).[22] Barry places trashy reading material, wine, and cigarettes at the

Figure 27. From *Picture This*. Copyright Lynda Barry. Used with permission from Drawn & Quarterly.

child's-eye level. Visually aligning Arna with access to and curiosity about bad influences captures a unique tension in Barry's oeuvre—her comics are *about* childhood but not necessarily *for* children, even though they are routinely shelved in the young adult section of libraries. Noting this contrast, Hillary Chute observes that Barry's *One! Hundred! Demons!* "evokes both artists' books and children's pop-up books, juxtaposing and rendering unstable, in this aspect as elsewhere, the discernible line between childhood and adulthood."[23] Likewise, in the opening to *Blabber, Blabber, Blabber,* Barry makes sure to remind readers: "THIS BOOK *IS NOT FOR KIDS* UNLESS THEY HAVE FOUND IT AND ARE *sneak-reading it* BECAUSE YOU DIDN'T HIDE IT WELL ENOUGH FROM KIDS."[24] Her question in *Picture This*, "Was it a book for kids or grown-ups?" illustrates how the adult preoccupation with drinking in children's materials is a red herring that directs attention away from childhood's proximity to inappropriate experiences, objects, and texts. Throughout her work, Barry rejects the fiction that bad influences in books could harm youth more than the violence of everyday life.

Barry exploits the tension around audience—that her comics are about children but not for them—as a resource for subversive humor. She describes her comics as a blend of "funny/not-funny," often tackling taboo topics like sexual violence and then layering her graphic narratives over with "just off-the-wall stuff, funny and off-beat."[25] Indeed, as Chute notes, Barry "is peerless at offering a world in which trouble is never skirted but levity can remain."[26] In a special issue of the journal *Iris* on women and humor, Barry reminds readers that "in humor, a person who normally shouldn't have power is quick-witted enough to take the whole thing" and that comedy allows us to see "how the system works."[27] Toggling between a childlike view of the world and an adult perspective on misogyny, Barry uses drinking child humor to critique lessons that naturalize the link between intoxication and sexual violence.

Rather than a substance that differentiates the child's experience from the adult's, alcohol in Barry's comics fuses age groups into a third space that is unregulated by chronology, punishment, or redemption. At times, affinities and alliances are even built between adults and children through stories of intoxication. Barry's comic "Sneaking Out" exemplifies this (see Figure 28).[28] The title, "Sneaking Out," suggests a rebellious adolescent activity; however, the first frame shows a father running away in the dark from a party thrown to celebrate his sobriety. "Sneaking Out" is about the adventures of both Maybonne Mullen and her father. Maybonne and her friend Cindy Ludermyer make a break for it after her dad's party, meeting other kids at a rope swing at

Figure 28. From "Sneaking Out" in *Drawn and Quarterly: Twenty-Five Years of Contemporary Cartooning, Comics, and Graphic Novels.* Copyright Lynda Barry. Used with permission from Drawn & Quarterly.

2 A.M. Each teen partygoer is to "bring inches of every kind of booze" to mix.[29] Things have gone off the rails by the time the girls arrive. Maybonne describes the scene: "Patty Herzock was hanging off the rope swing in her bra and panties" and everyone seems to be in their underwear. Maybonne confesses to the reader, "I was drunk and everyone was drunk. Tom Donato started Frenching me and when I looked around, everyone was Frenching everyone else."[30]

Tom and Maybonne go deeper into the woods. Maybonne narrates: "He kept taking my hand and putting it in his underwear. I kept not doing it. He kept saying, 'please please' and finally I touched it for about one minute then he sat up and barfed."[31] Barry draws Tom bent over, vomit spewing (see Figure 28), and in the following frames her comedic timing is impeccable as the pace and rhythm of the drinking jokes portray the aftermath of a party. Maybonne almost throws up, too, then starts to cry. When she finds Cindy Ludermyer, Cindy's crying, too, "because she barfed out her retainer and couldn't find it."[32] Drinking, sex, crying, and throwing up combine for comic effect. Barry claims gross-out humor, typically associated with male comics and the juvenile humor of men, as part of young women's experience, and in so doing refuses to pathologize girl drinkers.

It is in this state of intoxication that Maybonne bonds with her father, who she finds in the A&W parking lot on her way home. "'Hi Dad,' I said and I threw up."[33] Her father takes her to the gas station bathroom to clean up and buys her a cup of coffee. "'We're both in the doghouse' he said. And he didn't ask me nothing and I didn't ask him nothing. Except he did ask me if I smoked and he did give me a cigarette."[34] As they smoke and talk, her father confesses that he drinks alcohol to cope with everyday life—working for Mr. Ludermyer is killing him and living with Maybonne's grandma drives him nuts. When he drops his daughter home on his way out of town, she tells the reader that her father gave three pieces of advice: "Tell grandma not to worry, tell my sister he loved her, and for me to chew aspirin for my hangover."[35] Barry's teen drinking stories are not moralistic tales of addiction.

This is also the case in her long-running syndicated *Ernie Pook's Comeek*, of which Maybonne is a part. The strip "follows the inner world of children, but it's not *Peanuts*: This is a world of alcoholic parents, sadistic bullies, inept teachers and a stint or two in juvie."[36] Barry's adolescent heroines steal wine from parents and from synagogues; they drink the cheap stuff and the concoctions they make from whatever they can find give the reader a headache just thinking about it. In "Our Incredible Party," Barry encapsulates the euphoria of drinking and the agony of a hangover. The strip begins as Maybonne lies in bed with her younger sister Marlys who says: "You drank wine."

Maybonne replies: "Don't talk to me. And don't move the bed." Marlys, the voice of discipline: "You're a juvenile delinquent." Maybonne's hangover is the result of a night out in which her friend Brenda scored three bottles of Boone's Farm Apple wine by standing outside a store and asking "all guys with beards" to buy it for them. By the time they get to the keg party, it has been busted, and so not much transpires after they get drunk. They throw up and lie down in the schoolyard near the portables until "we could walk straight and talk straight so we could all go home and get screamed at by our moms and then lay in bed and swear we will never do it again."[37]

Barry begins the strip with teen ruin rather than innocence. It is set at the chronological end of a night of drinking. Maybonne nurses her hangover in bed, tortured by her annoying little sister, as she recollects her "incredible party." That she goes back in time detaches vulnerability from childhood—there is no state of innocence for Maybonne to return to or for her to breach. Marlys recites a cautionary lesson of the drinking curriculum: "Now I lay me down to sleep I'm sorry God but my sisters a wino." Maybonne tells her to *shut up*—not because she wants to debate the wino part, but because she wants to sleep. We know, too, that Maybonne has sworn before not to drink, but will ultimately go out again. In this strip and others, Barry's humorous portrayals of drinking girls destigmatize intoxication, normalizing it as an ordinary part of coming of age.

At other times, Barry's scenes of girlhood drunkenness tilt toward the un-funny as she uses the comics form to critique drunkenness as an excuse for sexual violence.[38] In "More Boys," Barry revisits the sneaking out plot. Maybonne says: "Cindy Ludermyer is so into guys and guys are so into Cindy Ludermyer but not in the for real way. They are into her in the giant boob way" and that "Both girls and boys have said it: Slut, Slut, Slut." Cindy Ludermyer plans to sneak out to the rope swing at 1 A.M. to meet some new boys from the Catholic school. Maybonne is joined by her little sister, Marlys.[39] In the next strip, "It's Cool," Maybonne is greeted by two of the boys who tell her "there's just some things that men have to keep to themselves."[40] Cindy's sweater is on a rock, but she is nowhere to be found. Barry relies on the reader's knowledge of the joint lessons in rape culture and the drinking curriculum: that it is dangerous for girls to consume alcohol, especially outside of the home and especially with boys. In this version, there is no vomit or gross-out humor to shore up the comic vignette.

Maybonne states that the sight of the sweater starts her "freaking out for me and freaking out for Cindy, who loves Boones Farm Apple wine and there's the bottle empty on its side by the rock."[41] One of the Catholic boys, Dan, emerges from the forest brushing his pants off and wiping his mouth and tells

Maybonne: "Don't freak out, man. It's cool. It's cool." Barry doesn't represent sexual assault explicitly, rather she leads the reader to infer violence in the gutters of the strip. The altercation is reflected in Marlys' glasses as is Dan's forceful attempt to keep Maybonne from going after Cindy. In the following strip, "She wanted it She wanted it," the narrative details what Marlys saw: "She saw those guys and Cindy Ludermyer. She hid in the bushes and watched Cindy pushing on the guy and the guy pushing on Cindy. And it was Marlys that threw the rock. 'You Little Bitch!' is what the guy called my sister. It was her first time of that name. He caught her and dragged her and said to his friends 'What are we going to do now?'"[42]

Barry visualizes the unspeakable, how the drinking curriculum instructs girls that they are "asking for it" when they drink for pleasure or when they instigate drinking. The boys, too, perform a gendered curriculum, but intoxication provides them cover and bonding. Through this graphic feminist pedagogy, Barry also teaches allyship—it is the young Marlys who throws a rock to protect her sister and Cindy.[43] The tale of gang rape is witnessed by, held onto, and resolved by the girls themselves. In *Tainted Witness*, Leigh Gilmore argues that girls and women face a credibility deficit, especially when they speak out about sexual violence, and that blame routinely shifts onto them and away from those who do harm.[44] The girls have internalized this knowledge and navigate a crisis in which no one will help or believe them. Maybonne tells the reader that "Cindy was so drunk. She was crying. Laying in the leaves and the sticks and crying. I kicked the guys leg who was holding me and he knocked me in the head. Two guys ran. One guy pointed at Cindy and said 'she started it.' And held his cig pack to me like 'did I want one.'" He points to Marlys who is standing by Maybonne not moving: "You tell anybody and the world will know what a slut Cindy is. You want that?"[45] Maybonne informs the reader: "Those boys got away with it. They got away with it. People say it was Cindy who caused the whole thing."[46]

Narrating the aftermath in "It's Nothing," Maybonne says: "I still want her to tell the police on those guys. She says it's all ready too late. No one would believe her now. 'But you got witnesses!' I say. 'I saw and Marlys Saw!' She said who was going to believe me and Marlys? Then she's quiet and when I look over, her shoulders are shaking" (see Figure 29).[47] Cindy submerges her pain as she takes in gendered lessons about drunkenness that insist that she is to blame. "They'll say I started everything because of it was me that scored the wine and said where to meet . . . people will say she is trying to wreck their future."[48]

Visually, an interplay exists between the girl who is frozen in her bed and an awful trauma she's trying to process with Maybonne. Barry's panels are

Figure 29. From *It's So Magic*. Copyright Lynda Barry. Used with permission from Drawn & Quarterly.

continuous, and the gutter slows time as Cindy's feet move back and forth. The words tell the truth about a long and difficult post-traumatic future, and the gutter suggests bodily immobility. The panels work in an affective mode, and they hold the story that she is trying to get out. The gutter is the space of inertia. Situated in the space of girlhood, a bedroom complete with stuffed toys and a ruffled pillow, the panels visualize how traumatic knowledge works. Certain lessons are simultaneously remembered and forgotten, and alcohol plays a role in that knowing. Barry writes "I cringe when people talk about the resiliency of children. It's a hope adults have about the nature of a child's inner life, that it's simple, that what can be forgotten can no longer affect us. But it is forgetting."[49] The teen girl's testimony is consigned to the landscape of girlhood, the bedroom, unspeakable and unbelievable outside of its walls.

There is no punch line. For Marlys, what she saw is unrepresentable (see Figure 30). In "If you want to Know Teenagers by Marlys," the last panel written in childish handwriting reads: "Sorry for no picture. I saw something I can't even draw it. Don't try to guess it. Just forget it."[50] Barry visualizes how girls come to internalize one of the most insidious lessons of the drinking curriculum that continues to inform cases of sexual assault from Steubenville High to Stanford University. Alcohol may make girls vulnerable to sexual assault, but Barry highlights how the real danger rests in male entitlement, not with drinking. The boys who rape drunk girls aren't funny. Barry teaches us about permissible violence—who gets away with it under cover of drinking—and

Figure 30. From *It's so Magic*. Copyright Lynda Barry. Used with permission from Drawn & Quarterly.

exposes culturally codified associations between drinking and masculinity. Through her funny/un-funny humor she brings into view often hidden knowledge about both drinking girls and sexual abuse.

Barry's alternative lessons remain radical in this politically fraught time when neo-temperance advocates attempt to tie #MeToo to abstinence, once again trying to enforce the idea that girls and women are to blame for sexual assault if they drink too much alcohol. In these frameworks, girls map onto women and all "girls" are assumed to be at risk. Headlines like "After Kavanaugh, #MeToo Should Launch a New Temperance Movement" suggest that debates about alcohol also structure gendered dynamics, and argue that to fight sexual assault we need to temper alcohol consumption.[51] Alcohol is a key element in the revival of neo-temperance activism that seeks to attach feminism to sobriety but is really regurgitating old lessons in the drinking curriculum that pathologize as promiscuous girls and women who drink, especially in public. Barry's illustrated novel *Cruddy* begins: "Do not blame the drugs. It was not the fault of the drugs." So, too, her comics advise: Do not blame the alcohol.[52]

William Elder provides the epigraph for this lesson: "Humor depends on the neighborhood it's born in." Drinking child humor was born in underground comix and childhood was redrawn by artists outside of the mainstream. Through a takedown of cuteness and love of the profane Elder, Spiegelman, Barry, and others created visions of young people in which innocence is not the dominant mode of representation. The next lesson, "Mommy Needs a Cocktail," continues the examination of the links between humor, intoxication, and childhood.

Lesson Five
Mommy Needs a Cocktail

The final chapter of Charles Jewett's *The Youth's Temperance Lecturer* includes a terrifying tale of a little girl who is "so badly burned that she lived but a few hours." The nameless, hapless youngster's clothes catch on fire when an inebriate mother leaves her two daughters at home to go fill up a bottle of rum (see Figure 31). The sister and a neighbor are too late to save the girl. Writes Jewett:

> O! 'twas an awful sight,
> To see that wretched girl,
> As round her brow, o'er her tresses light,
> The scorching flames did curl.
> And dreadful on the ear
> Rung her cry of agony,
> And her sister's shriek of more than fear,
> As the fire streamed red on high.
> Their mother loved the cup,
> And alone had left them there;
> She saw not the deadly fire stream up,
> And heard not the shriek of despair.[1]

The child burned alive illustrates the lethal irresponsibility of the mother caused by her insatiable desire for alcohol. We have reached the final lesson in the drinking curriculum, "Mommy Needs a Cocktail." Children's dependency and agency overlap when drinking mothers are present, thus expressing social fantasies, including violent ones, about a mother's relation to her children.

Figure 31. Charles Jewett, *The Youth's Temperance Lecturer* (1841). Courtesy, Harvard Library.

In Jewett's temperance tale, the absence of the rum-loving mother in the illustration is notable as it contrasts with horrifyingly realistic illustrations of the drunken, abusive father discussed in Lesson One of this book. The scene teaches as much about gender as it does about the effects of liquor. The scrubbing of the drunken mother from the picture aligns with the Women's Christian Temperance Union's depiction of women as the wholesome victims of drunken men in their campaigns for temperance. Thus, "when the public connected women and alcohol, two images predominated: the white-clad 'temperance ladies' of the WCTU, and the women they sought to protect—wives, mothers, and daughters. An inebriated woman was a less common and distinctly more stigmatized image, synonymous with loose morals, sexual promiscuity, and ruined motherhood."[2] The mother's love of the cup codes her desire as it takes her out of the private space of the home into the public sphere to fill her bottle. The gendered lesson of Jewett's tale maps onto the campaigns of the WCTU and other "drys" who sought to construct white middle- and upper-middle-class women's drinking, particularly outside the home, as contemptible.[3]

Yet, the mother's absence belies the presence of drinking mothers. In her global history of women and alcohol, Mallory O'Meara writes that women's drinking took place on the sly. "Society demanded that they serve as paragons of morality, so women had to get sneaky. Upper-class wives held so-called tea parties, where the participants delicately sipped sherry or gin from beautiful teacups. Gin cordials (liqueurs made with gin, sweeteners, and flavorings) were wildly popular among women, either purchased or homemade."[4] The WCTU's moral campaign against drinking was also anti-immigrant, and policing white affluent women's consumption of alcohol "stemmed from fears of race suicide."[5] Eugenicist theories mapped neatly onto medicalized discourses of alcoholism as hereditary. Mothers' addiction to alcohol would cause their off-spring to deteriorate. Exemplifying this belief, the popular nineteenth-century patent medicine, Mrs. Lydia E. Pinkham's Vegetable Compound, used the tag-line "health of woman is the hope of the race."

Paradoxically, Pinkham's patent medicine included fifteen percent alcohol and was marketed as a treatment for the pain of menstruation, childbirth, and menopause. Pinkham and her family endorsed temperance, claiming alcohol as a medicinal element and a preservative for the compound.[6] The boozy mixture, and others like it, were touted as a healthier alternative to the more feminine substance of choice, opium. Long before the marketing of minor tranquilizers like the brand Miltown in the mid-1950s, or of wine in the 2010s, affluent white women before 1900 were the "principal users of opiates, which were available over the counter and by mail order"; Sears Roebuck sold the Bayer Co.'s kit for $1.50 which included a syringe, two needles, two vials of heroin and a case.[7] If drinking in public in the nineteenth century was an activity associated with white masculinity, using opium in the home was linked to white femininity.

Alcohol was also a substance in medicines that mothers gave to their children. As the social value of children shifted from economically useful to "emotionally priceless," makers of patent medicines used children as "objects of sentiment" to sell their products.[8] One of the most powerful examples is Mrs. Winslow's Syrup. First marketed in the U.S. in 1845 as "the mother's friend," the concoction was a mix of morphine and alcohol. Its label pictured cute children and happy mothers together enjoying the benefits of a dose and a promise that it "soothes the child; gives rest to the mother" (see Figure 32). Advertised in magazines and newspapers, as well as in periodicals for children such as The Youth's Companion, soothing syrups were ubiquitous. On an exemplary trade card for Mrs. Winslow's syrup, it is hard to distinguish whether the mother is high, drunk, or simply napping. The young mother nods off, hallucinating her infant as a cherub, metaphorically sky high, dreaming of the heavens and angelic children. After a dose, the child has shape-shifted from a wild tyrant (as the discarded dolls on the chair and floor suggest) to a languid tot. The angelic imagery is even more disturbing

Figure 32. 1875 trade card for Mrs. Winslow's Soothing Syrup. Artist Unknown. Printed by Hatch Lith. Co. Courtesy of Philadelphia Museum of Art: The William H. Helfand Collection, 1993, 1993-105-20.

when considering that articles in *The New York Times* and the *American Journal of Pharmacy* regularly sounded alarms about how deadly these syrups could be.[9]

Likewise, Duffy's Malt Whiskey was sold in both bars and drugstores and made claims that it cured everything from consumption to malaria. A trade card from 1889 pictures three young children: "Our mothers use malt whiskey as a tonic." On the flip side, the mothers are pictured along with the slogan, "Every true mother needs it." The mothers address the reader: "Don't you think Duffy's pure malt agrees with us? It is absolutely pure & wholesome. Try it yourself" (see Figures 33 and 34). Using testimonials from children to sell sweetened whiskey to mothers reveals a history that has been hidden from view. Duffy's Malt Whiskey and other products that use the child to sell liquor counters a cultural dogma that insists that the child's innocence and alcohol's depravity reside in separate spheres.

These everyday images played a part in manufacturing fantasies for and about mothers. As an advertisement for Pabst Tonic in a 1914 edition of *Cosmopolitan* put it, "Motherhood is the crowning joy of a woman's life."[10] Bonding between mother and child dominates these visuals even as the product being sold undercuts that message, acknowledging the affective contradictions

Figure 33. Duffy Malt Whiskey Company (1881). Warshaw Collection of Business Americana, Archives Center, National Museum of American History, Smithsonian Institution

Figure 34. Duffy Malt Whiskey Company. Warshaw Collection of Business Americana, Archives Center, National Museum of American History, Smithsonian Institution

inherent in mothering: joy and dissatisfaction, affection and aggression. Advertisements picture cherry-cheeked, blonde, blue-eyed babies who look out tenderly at the viewer, sitting calmly beside their mother who gazes at the tot adoringly (see Figure 35). Meanwhile at the bottom of the picture sits a bottle of alcoholic tonic, larger than the baby. This niche marketing makes liquor respectable under the cover of virtuous motherhood.

Such ads visually corroborate a shift in the understanding of children from useful labor to precious objects during the late 1800s, which changed a mother's orientation to and responsibility for her child.[11] Repositioned as subjects that required special clothes, toys, and care brought to light moral and ethical issues around children's treatment as the highly publicized 1874 case of 10-year-old Mary Ellen Wilson who was beaten regularly by her adoptive mother demonstrates. These staged and stagnant scenes of motherly adoration hide from view the potential violence that alcohol animates.

Violence, Alcohol, and Mothering

Amidst the many depravities pictured in British artist William Hogarth's famous 1751 etching, "Gin Lane," a baby falls to their death while an inebriated mother reaches for her snuff, too drunk to notice (see Figure 36). Caught in mid-air, mouth agape in terror, the cherubic child plummets down the stairwell. Other tots suffer similar fates: a mother tilts a glass of gin down the throat of a babe in arms, a drunken reveler carries a lifeless school-aged body on a stake, a small child lies alone on the ground as their mother is placed half naked into a coffin. The trouble caused by gin, or "mother's ruin," is further underscored by Hogarth's companion piece and a visual argument for moderation, "Beer Street," in which no children are visible—the vulnerable youngsters presumably tucked away in a safe domestic space with a sober maternal figure and no keys to the liquor cabinet.

Hogarth based "Gin Lane," on the case of Judith Defour who in 1734 strangled her 2-year-old daughter and left her in a ditch. After this, she sold the child's clothes and used the money to buy gin. Defour was convicted of murder and hanged. As Patrick Dillion observes, Hogarth's visual argument was gendered, drawing "the symbol of everything a woman ought not to be. She was the degeneration of mother into child-killer, beauty into something filthy, wife into shameless whore."[12] Hogarth's mother is the embodiment of "mother's ruin," a powerful graphic organizer about the cultural associations between childhood, violence, alcohol, and motherhood.

Considered alongside Jewett's erasure of the drunken mother and the marketing of alcohol as the medicinal aid for good mothers in visual culture,

Figure 35. Lydia E. Pinkham's Vegetable Compound (1912). Warshaw Collection of Business Americana, Archives Center, National Museum of American History, Smithsonian Institution

Figure 36. William Hogarth, "Gin Lane" (1751).

incitements to imbibe or abstain work hand in hand to construct the fiction that a woman's primary role is motherhood. Concerns about where, what, and how mothers drink never really disappear because cultural anxieties about gender are never settled and women remain primary caregivers. Some feminist critics suggest that after women make headway or take up space in public life, new "epidemics" emerge. For instance, as second-wave feminists introduced Title IX and agitated for equal rights, concerns about motherhood and drinking surfaced. In *Her Best Kept Secret*, journalist Gabrielle Glaser observes that

> [t]he discovery in the 1970s and '80s that alcohol had dangerous effects on fetuses (called fetal alcohol syndrome, FAS), while legitimate and alarming, escalated concerns about women's drinking as a wider social problem. A century after the founding of the WCTU, the outcry over FAS turned attention solely on female imbibers. Suddenly, there was intense focus on women's drinking habits, regardless of whether they were pregnant.[13]

Mapping onto Glaser's observations, in 1980, Marian Sandmaier published *The Invisible Alcoholics* and chronicled both the cultural stereotyping and the denial of alcoholic women.[14] Sandmaier marked the hypocrisy of concern about mothers' drinking and recovery programs that catered to men; mothers, for instance, needed childcare to go into treatment.

Likewise, alcoholic mothers are an uncommon sight in children's literature. One notable exception is the now out-of-print informational picture book by Kevin Kenny and Helen Krull, *Sometimes My Mom Drinks Too Much*. Published in 1980, the text reflects rising concerns about women's drinking and folds into discourses of the "new temperance" movement of that decade. The book is based in a disease model of addiction. H. Neidengard, M.D. chief of service, Cabrini alcoholism program, New York City writes the foreword for parents and teachers, and the text asserts that the mother "has a sickness, like measles or chicken pox. It's called alcoholism."[15] The front cover pictures a blonde schoolgirl standing in the foreground. The child is harmed psychologically rather than physically by the drinking mother who sits at a kitchen table sipping a glass of red wine, with half a decanter left to consume. While the book is meant to build empathy for the alcoholic mother, it also became the butt of a joke.

In 2017, Jimmy Fallon included *Sometimes My Mom Drinks Too Much* in his "Do Not Read" book list sketch on *The Tonight Show*.[16] In his bit, Fallon shares a full-page spread that pictures the drunken mother who has fallen to the floor while carrying her daughter's birthday cake (see Figure 37). When Fallon reads the text and shows the image, the audience erupts with laughter. Fallon repeats incredulously that this is *a children's book*. Fallon's joke hinges on the misogyny embedded in the drinking curriculum, the ways in which we equate a woman's "drunkenness with a threatening abdication of her social role."[17] It is also the case that the joke is on Fallon and the audience. Intoxication is a common trope in children's materials, it's only when an image—the drunk mother in this case—disrupts this transparent curriculum that we see it.

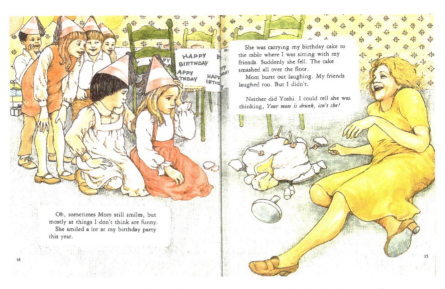

Figure 37. Kevin Kenny and Helen Krull, *Sometimes My Mom Drinks Too Much* (1980).

That is, the book stands out as extraordinary not because drunkenness is rare in children's materials, but because across time the drunken mother has been hidden from view.

Published the same year, cartoonist Lynda Barry in her 1980 strip "Girls and Boys" (first published in the *Chicago Reader*), offers a more nuanced picture. Sipping on a martini, a well-heeled mother tells her child to get into pajamas before their father gets home (see Figure 38). After this piece of motherly advice, she promptly passes out onto the floor, her eye marked with an x and martini glass toppled. The gutter confronts the reader as the next panel could lean into humor or it could turn to horror. Like Jewett's graphic narrative that opened this lesson, Barry takes a turn toward the latter as the child screams at her parent to "wake up!" Focalized through the child's perspective and their emotional distress, Barry places them in the upper corner of the image, standing over the adult. In the last frame, the child holds the mother's limp fingers, instructing the father (who remains out of the frame) to "leave her alone Daddy."[18] Barry both exposes maternal drinking and refuses to pathologize it. The SLAM! of the door when the father enters coupled with the urgency of the mother and child suggests a violent patriarch and emphasizes the "social and political conditions which might underlie female drinking."[19]

Barry illustrates how drinking "geographies are gendered, with men's heavy drinking tending to take place in public whilst women's heavy drinking

Figure 38. From "Girls and Boys" in *Blabber Blabber Blabber*. Copyright Lynda Barry. Used with permission from Drawn & Quarterly.

is more private and solitary."[20] The strip, like nineteenth-century graphic narratives including Cruikshank's *The Bottle* and Jewett's *The Youth's Temperance Lecturer*, foregrounds domestic violence and the precariousness of women and children in the white middle-class family, albeit for different ends. Here, the horrors of maternal drinking are not meant to reform the adult, but to express the violence that adults inflict on children, whether drunk or not. Barry brings things we don't want to see, the drunken, passed-out mother, out of the gutter and into the frame. The child's terror underscores that there's nothing funny or girlish about women overconsuming hard liquor. Importantly, Barry highlights how childhood agency might be less a choice than a consequence of violence.

That alcohol is most harmful to pregnant women is embedded in the danger label that first appeared on alcoholic drinks in 1989: "1) According to the

Surgeon General, women should not drink during pregnancy because of the risk of birth defects 2) Consumption of alcoholic beverages impairs your ability to drive a car or operate machinery, and may cause health problems." The warning might have included other information, like that the consumption of alcohol by non-pregnant people, especially those between 20–39 years of age, puts them at risk of high blood pressure, stroke, and death.[21] The label reiterates the gendered lessons of the drinking curriculum around women and their place in it as good mothers. Regardless of all the cautionary tales from Hogarth to Jewett to the U.S. Surgeon General, mothers continue to drink.

Humor and The Commodification of Resentment

Fast forward to the aughts when women reclaimed intoxication as an antidote to the trials of motherhood. Books like Christie Mellor's 2004 *The Three-Martini Play Date: A Practical Guide to Happy Parenting* and Stefanie Wilder-Taylor's *Sippy Cups are Not for Chardonnay* and *Naptime is the New Happy Hour* appeared.[22] Popular media outlets including *The New York Times* began to take note of the trend with headlines that included "Cosmopolitan Moms: Adult Beverages Find Their Place at Children's Play Dates" which chronicled happy hours in tony neighborhoods.[23] One of the most familiar characters to emerge out of this trend was the white wine mom, and by the mid-2010s wine mom memes, TikTok, and blog posts were commonplace on the internet. However, the wine mom phenomenon didn't appear out of thin air.[24]

Like patent medicines in the nineteenth century, wine was marketed to women in the decades after Prohibition and then directly to mothers—as a 2011 lawsuit between two vintners about which could use the word "Mommy" on a wine label underscores.[25] Cheryl Durzy, creator of MommyJuice wine, stated in a 2013 interview that researching online she found "a number of different groups on Facebook like, 'OMG I Need a Glass of Wine or I'm Going to Kill My Kids,' or 'Moms Who Need Wine,' that have over half a million [members]."[26] Her wine brand MommyJuice was aimed at this demographic. Yet, when trying to sell her product she got some pushback. One distributor refused to carry MommyJuice because it sounded "like breast milk"; another e-mailed Durzy to say, "shame on you. How could you make a wine that kids think is for them?" Codes of white women's wellness culture are hard to miss on the MommyJuice wine label, which features a woman sitting in a meditation pose juggling a computer, a house, kitchen utensils, and a teddy bear. By 2021, wine mom discourse could be "found in nearly every social media outlet and every store and across a wide range of products."[27] While wine moms have been the subject of much cultural debate, one of the underexamined features of drinking mom culture—vino or otherwise—is humor that upends cloying images of perfect motherhood while bringing sublimated resentments out into the open.

Humor is an escape valve, and a side effect of the decades-long marketing of alcohol and other mind-altering substances to suppress discontent in a capitalist framework that defines mothering as the natural enactment of maternal love rather than the unpaid labor that it is. This brand of comedy is ubiquitous and works in part by repurposing ordinary visual forms and material objects meant to evoke sentimental feelings about children or that reflect a nostalgia for childhood icons. For example, the greeting card, "You just had a baby!!!! Time to start drinking" takes the discursive undercurrents of nineteenth-century advertisements discussed earlier and uses them for satire (see Figure 39). The mother tries to look out at the viewer, while the demanding toddler physically pulls her attention away from her real object of pleasure, the martini in the bottom corner.

Intensive parenting is the child-rearing method du jour, and the contemporary tot is economically useless and emotionally exhausting.[28] Privileged twenty-first-century children demand their mother's resources of care, time, and freedom and the child's needs fall almost exclusively to women. As the Covid-19 pandemic made clear, mothers remain our culture's emotional vending machines, and we require them to have nothing but loving feelings toward their children.[29] In response, some women turned to humor. Countless examples appear on social media, in posts like "It's Mother's Day: Go Ahead and Get Shit Balls Drunk," and "Boxed Wine is Just a Juice Box for Mom." Mothers use alcohol and intoxication to sanction an outpouring of maternal animosity.

An exemplary TikTok video @charmingandmain uses the iconic 1939 film *The Wizard of Oz* for inspiration. A middle-aged white woman in a bathrobe speaks into the camera:

> I was pretty hopeful today was going to be a red glittery shoe day when in fact it is actually a squad of flying fucking monkeys day, so buckle up bitches it's going to be a bumpy ride.

As she speaks, she pours out a healthy dose from a magnum of Captain Morgan rum into a coffee mug. Hashtags include #mommyjuice, #wizardofoz, #momsover40, #capitanmorgan. Whether we find a mom drinking a coffee mug of Captain Morgan at 8:00 A.M. funny is immaterial. More importantly, texts associated with childhood are referenced and repurposed for laughs. In this case, a middle-aged mom in a bathrobe stands in for Dorothy Gale, tugging out and juxtaposing two affective strands, love and aversion. The red glittery

Figure 39. Drinking humor on a greeting card for a mother.

shoes evoke the sentiment that "there's no place like home" and the fantasy of make-believe, and the terrifying flying monkeys represent her current reality. She, like the Cowardly Lion, needs a bowl of liquid courage.

Drinking mom humor finds an additional outlet in parodies of material children's culture like the best-selling author, artist, and cartoonist Lisa Brown's *Baby Mix Me a Drink*.[30] A reviewer for *O, The Oprah Magazine* defines Brown's series "Baby Be of Use," which includes the titles *Baby Make Me Breakfast*, *Baby Fix My Car*, and *Baby Do My Banking* as "wish-fulfillment for wilting parents" that takes the "boredom out of board books."[31] The copy for *Baby, Mix Me a Drink* asks, "Are you a parent? Are you thirsty? Too many of us allow our infant sons and daughters to lay about idly napping, drinking milk, and sometimes 'turning over.' Why not have them mix you a cocktail? Thanks, Baby!" Each page includes a mixology template for different members of the family. The first is a martini for mama (see Figure 40).

Baby, Mix Me a Drink is in the form of a small board book, an object created to withstand what Walter Benjamin defined as the "despotic and dehumanized elements in children."[32] Additionally, like educational shape-recognition texts that purportedly teach babies to organize visual information, Brown inserts easily recognizable liquor brands, Bombay Sapphire distilled London dry gin and Martini dry vermouth. That the martini is the mother's drink tickles the viewer to question whether gin is mother's helper or mother's ruin as Hogarth pictured it. The baby serves the desires of the mother and brings her enjoyment, rather than the other way around. Brown foregrounds alcohol as pleasure and a baby that brings ease rather than misery.

Figure 40. *Baby Mix Me a Drink* © Lisa Brown 2005

The overlap between children's culture, motherhood, and drinking humor came to a head in 2012 in a surprising location: Nick Jr., Viacom's network geared to preschool children. Nick Jr. made its mark in 2000 with *Dora the Explorer*. The show's main character quickly became a target of alcohol-related jokes as evidenced by images of moms drinking alcohol out of Dora sippy cups, Dora the Explorer cocktail recipes, and the cartoon's spot in Lyranda Martin-Evans and Fiona Stevenson's *Reasons Mommy Drinks*.[33] Years after the release of *Dora*, Viacom tried to draw fresh viewers to Nick Jr., and released NickMom, an adult nighttime programming block that aired from 2012 to 2015. The title sequence for the show began with a crying baby, a schedule of packing lunch, and driving to afterschool activities, all while children aggressively shout "mom" at increasingly loud decibels; it ended with a martini glass.

NickMom's slogan was "Mother Funny." It was front-loaded with drinking and sex jokes and included comedy shows like Wilder-Taylor's *Parental Discretion* and *Instant Mom* starring Tia Mowry. From the beginning, NickMom met with trouble. The network advertised NickMom with the tagline, "see you there without the kids," however Nick Jr. was set to a default Eastern Time Zone schedule. This meant that in addition to the intended adult audience of moms in New York City watching at 10:00 P.M., toddlers on the west coast were simultaneously consuming sex jokes. Outraged parents condemned the block's programming and created a change.org petition as well as a now-defunct website cancelnickmom.com.[34] Most parents were "upset about the on-air content, which includes jokes about stoned TGI Fridays busboys, circumcision, grandma's vaginas, and lots and lots of sex."[35] Oddly, the outrage didn't extend to the centrality of alcohol to NickMom's brand or to the common-sense marketing of it as a form of self-care.

Moms were invited to pour themselves a glass of wine before sitting down to view NickMom programming. The network helpfully provided recipes for alcoholic drinks to consume while watching their shows (see Figure 41). Little objects of childhood—marbles, play hammers, toy trucks, mini umbrellas—adorn the NickMom cocktail recipe cards. A tiny, adorable dump truck, all round edges and bright colors, delivers a lime for the Ultimate Mom-Arita for mothers "who deserve yummy drinks too." The use-value of the toy is remade through the mother's desire. It, unlike actual children, has a purpose. The image is double-edged; it's the alcoholic beverage that begs to be picked up and cooed over, and the toy truck discarded after the lime is retrieved. The toy has been repurposed by the mother for cocktail hour and she's put it to use; trucks deliver limes while board books become coasters.

Yet, the truck's littleness codes the mother's drinking as diminutive. Marguerite Duras writes that "when a woman drinks, it's as if an animal were drinking,

Figure 41. NickMom cocktail recipe card, "The Ultimate Mom-Arita."

or a child. Alcoholism is scandalous in a woman, and a female alcoholic is rare, a serious matter. It's a slur on the divine in our nature."[36] The cultural logic of white motherhood demands that a mom's drinking be cute and harmless, a lesser form of male drinking. Women's drinks are sugary, childlike, weak, or girly. Proving the hardiness of these stereotypes, even women's drinking is infantilized as a "girls' night out." Sianne Ngai argues that as an aesthetic category, cuteness evokes a "surprisingly wide spectrum of feelings, ranging from tenderness to aggression that we harbor toward ostensibly subordinate and unthreatening commodities."[37] The outpouring of bad feelings about mothering in drinking humor taps into the darker side of cuteness that Ngai documents. The cute childhood object cuts two ways, it both invites the mother's ire and domesticates her pleasure.

That is, the repurposing of forms like baby board books and toys vivify childhood innocence and at the same time animate visions of the debauchery that might result from drinking. Shot glasses adorned with the cute likeness of Winnie the Pooh or Hello Kitty underscore this uneasy association between alcohol, childhood, and innocence. Benjamin theorized adult attachments to children's toys as an attempt to control their own worlds, observing that when "surrounded by a world of giants, children use play to create a world appropriate to their size. But the adult, who finds himself threatened by the real world and can find no escape, removes its sting by playing with its image in reduced form."[38] Drinking mom jokes delight in the violence of child's play and at the same time infantilize women through associations with the diminutive accouterments of childhood. Yet, as Anna Mae Duane writes, infantilization "is not a rhetorical club with which those in power simply disempower an individual by comparing him or her to a child. Rather, the structure of the child metaphor often changes the meanings of *both* terms."[39] Mothers become more child-like; children become more agentic. The cherubic child that peers out at the viewer in advertisements for patent medicines in the nineteenth-century morphs into the outwardly petulant and active children in the twenty-first.[40]

Children's commodities, those cute, cheerful, educational toys, simple board books, and mind-numbing cartoons like *Dora the Explorer*, like the images of cute children and their mothers in advertisements discussed earlier, obfuscate the reality of the emotional, economic, and physical labor of mothering. Drinking humor allows a temporary alteration of mood to safely vent and ultimately remain in the confines of normative white femininity. Linda Hutcheon argues that parody is "authorized transgression."[41] Indeed, the targets of intoxicated mom jokes and parodies are not universal childcare or equal pay, but rather the toys and stories manufactured by the childhood innocence industry that hide the realities of their care work. This humor is two-sided. It temporarily condones "bad" feelings to reveal a chasm between fantasies of motherhood enshrined in popular culture and that of real life and it is an outcome of a long history in which alcohol has been sold to women, especially white affluent women, as a tonic for mothering.

Final Exam

"To alcohol: The cause of, and solution to, all of life's problems."

— HOMER SIMPSON

Covid-19 brought concerns about substance abuse as well as jokes about day drinking and "the hellscape that is pandemic parenting" into the limelight.[1] On May 9, 2020, *Saturday Night Live* aired the musical sketch "Let Kids Drink."[2] Fittingly, given the number of women who quit their jobs to take care of schoolchildren, the broadcast took place the day before Mother's Day.[3] Lyrics included:

> If they got a little buzz on would it really be that bad? They'll be happier and funnier and they'll fall asleep by six.

> They used to give kids whiskey to help them fall asleep, so a teeny tiny White Claw is just a babysitter on the cheap.

The camera shots capture school-aged children drinking beer, a baby who can barely lift a wine bottle, and youngsters passed out surrounded by empty alcohol containers. Josh Gad, the voice of Disney's character Olaf, sings, "Give kids drinks. Disney said it's fine. Here's a bedtime story it's vodka, soda, lime." A line appears on the screen "Disney *Not approved by Disney; multiple lawsuits pending." A child sips out of a Mickey Mouse martini glass. "Let kids drink . . . It's not like they can drive. Just 1 drink, 2 if they've been good." Of course, this is make-believe drinking and the children in the video are safe and sober. But the *SNL* writers draw on the long tradition of drinking humor documented in this book in which drunk children are funny and children drive adults to drink. Through comedy, the skit confronts a public health crisis in which parents and children are stuck together in the home: parents play the role of teacher, kids are found in adult workspaces, and everyone's parenting is literally on view. Parents struggle to cope by drinking more, and as they do so they dissolve—for comedic purposes—a profound boundary about responsibility.

Nonetheless, after the SNL skit aired, a controversy erupted on social media. Some viewers found the images of drunk babies, toddlers, and school-aged children "freaking hysterical" while others argued that they sent "the wrong message for kids" and that the creators failed to consider a person's "abusive relationship with alcohol."[4] If there's one takeaway from the drinking curriculum it's this: arguments about whether a text is appropriate or inappropriate for kids are a deflection that upholds the status quo. Remarkably, the blowback is less about the actual needs of families during the pandemic when work and schooling moved into domestic spaces, but, instead, directs pre-made censure (especially about women and mothers) that is conservative during a crisis that is begin satirized, not minimized. The outrage deflects concern away from the pressures of the pandemic on parents, especially mothers.

If you recognized the cluster of responses identified in this book (social problems mischaracterized as the moral failing of women, the curious presence of drinking children as an index to these problems, ambivalence about the demands of child-rearing expressed in humor), you have mastered the lessons on horror and humor in the drinking curriculum and are ready for the final exam. Did you notice that the jokes in the SNL skit are predictable? The association of infants with intoxicated behavior—"babies look drunk anyway. And burp and puke just like I would,"—echoes nineteenth-century discourses linking childishness and drunkenness. The verse about White Claw being a babysitter on the cheap touches on the marketing of dangerous "medicinal" concoctions to mothers for profit. The Disney joke is less outrageous than it first appears because tipsy characters are present from the company's inception and continue into the present. In 2021, for example, Disney Plus' executive producer asked *The Simpsons* team to create an animated short that would "cram as many of the company's franchise characters as possible into Moe's Tavern,"[5] which resulted in "The Simpsons in Plusaversary." When choosing Disney characters, the company didn't want "anyone who is a role model for young kids like Belle to be drinking." In the end, they picked Goofy because he "has been portrayed with a kid in the past, which made it OK for him to enjoy those Duffs with Homer" (see Figure 42).[6]

What the SNL sketch exposed through humor is one of the take-aways from this book: If there is a hard line to be drawn between adulthood and child-

Figure 42. "The Simpsons in Pulsaversary" (2021). Disney Plus / Matt Groening.

hood, alcohol is not it. As of this writing, adult drinking paraphernalia imprinted with references to childhood, from *The Cat in the Hat* wine glasses that read "I will drink wine here or there I will drink wine anywhere" to Disney princess shot glasses, are everywhere. Mixology books like Nick Perry and Paul Rosser's *Drink Me: Curious Cocktails from Wonderland* nod to children's classics, and rules for drinking games based on any number of kids' shows are easy to find.[7] These links between childishness and intoxication are so ubiquitous that we fail to see them as noteworthy. With the rise of the #sobercurious movement, bars now offer artisanal mocktails, yet articles on this new sobriety rarely mention that one of the most iconic mocktails, the Shirley Temple, was first created for the 10-year-old actress so she could drink alongside her parents and other cocktail-sipping celebrities.[8] Finally, alcohol-inspired products continue to find their way into the nursery, including the "Chill Baby Li'l Lager Baby Bottle" which looks like a beer bottle and "will let tykes kick back their favorite formula."[9]

Significantly, one of the most powerful and insidious teachers disseminating the lessons of the drinking curriculum is the liquor industry, which continues to pivot and profit from selling alcohol to people of all ages. The use of children to sell medicinal malts in the nineteenth century, product placement in family films, and wine marketing to mothers exemplify the flexibility of beverage corporations as they continue to educate us about alcohol by proliferating opportunities to imbibe. We all pay the price, not because liquor companies are inherently bad, but because a long-standing cultural fetishization of childhood innocence allows us to avoid confronting our paradoxical relationship with alcohol and youth. Liquor companies tap into fantasies about playfulness and pleasure. They represent intoxication as both carefree and consequence-free, an association that resonates particularly with nostalgia for childhood as a protected space of suspended harm. But even an understanding of the sticky tentacles of capitalism does not explain away alcohol's consistent proximity to childhood.

The drinking curriculum reveals a surprising archive of comedic violence, scenes of intoxication that rely on the child, childishness, and the childlike for legibility. This humor encompasses countless slapstick depictions of drunk children and childish drunkards, the parodical defacement of cute children's books and toys, and cutting jokes expressed via inebriated and overworked caretakers, be they the animated Drunk Stork or the working mother. Horror and humor overlap in the drinking curriculum. Nineteenth-century temperance fictions picture horrific scenes of child abuse that reflect an entrenched misopedia, Looney Tunes/Merry Melodies Drunk Stork cartoons express disdain for children and anxieties about child-rearing through repeatedly putting babies in harm's way, in *E.T.* the script leans into the horror genre as a school-age child becomes unknowingly drunk when possessed by an alien being, and in wine mom culture, resentment of mothering and children are deployed through the re-purposing of children's texts and toys for alcohol consumption. In the drinking curriculum, humor in which the child and alcohol are pictured sanctions the expression of violence; it is rule-breaking, fantasy, and a relief valve. Horror and humor operate together in the drinking curriculum, revealing broad anxieties both about alcohol and children that balance on a razor's edge of pleasure and fear.

This book ends where it began, with a child reaching for a drink alongside an adult, not in the sepia-tinted illustrations of the nineteenth-century, but in a jaunty jingle from an *SNL* skit about pandemic parenting. Whether the drinking curriculum animates concerns about violence in the white middle-class family that the temperance movement exposed, traffic fatalities, the pains of parenting, or the inadequacy of the public health system during Covid-19, alcohol is an index of harm. When alcohol and childhood share the spotlight, we confront ideas about who's vulnerable and who isn't, who has agency and who lacks it, what is socially acceptable and what isn't, and for which people. Graphic narratives of intoxication express anxieties about youth—as both subjects to protect and to fear.

Childhood adheres to cultural understandings of alcohol and embodiments of intoxication even as adults protest that it should not. Ultimately, what we learn from the nineteenth-century temperance movement onward is that the definition of childhood at the drinking curriculum's center is hard to pin down: the child is a teetotaler and a potential addict, an innocent and a knowledgeable partaker, a victim and a savior. In answer to the question posed at the outset of this book, "Why do we need the child to teach us about alcohol?" the answer has been in front of us all along. Drinking culture is children's culture.

Acknowledgments

The idea for this book began in 2015 while drinking at a bar with Naomi Hamer, Derritt Mason, and Lisa Weems. At first, an academic study of alcohol in children's culture seemed an irreverent joke, yet my research snowballed into these pages.

The drinking curriculum is highly visual, and this text includes many images. I am grateful to Lisa Brown for allowing me to use an illustration from her book *Baby, Mix Me a Drink*, Drawn and Quarterly for permitting the reproduction of images from Lynda Barry's comics, La Pastèque for granting permission to reproduce an image from *Louis Undercover*, and the Edward Gorey Charitable Trust for use of the "Z is for Zillah" illustration. Thank you to Hillary Chute for generously sharing a high-resolution version of "Visiting the Grandparents." I also thank the librarians and staff at the American Antiquarian Society, the Baldwin Library of Historical Children's Literature, the National Museum of American History, the Philadelphia Museum of Art, the University of Washington, and the Widener Library at Harvard University, as they facilitated the reproduction of many of the pictures in this book. Simon Fraser University provided essential financial support through the SFU publication fund that covered permissions and production costs.

Richard Morrison championed this project from its inception, and his expertise, humor, and steady advice made working on this book together a delight. I thank the editorial and production team, especially Kem Crimmins and Eric Newman, at Fordham University Press for their professionalism and care in bringing *The Drinking Curriculum* to publication. I appreciate the anonymous reviewers who offered insights and critiques that made this book stronger. Courtney Adams provided a close reading of this manuscript and I am grateful for her edits. I am especially indebted to the talented Mark Lerner for his outstanding cover design.

Many colleagues influenced this book by giving feedback, offering suggestions, providing support, and inviting me to share my ideas, including Kristine Alexander, Laurie Anderson, Michelle Anya Anjirbag, Kate Capshaw, Brigitte Fielder, Kathleen Forrester, Adam Greteman, Annette Henry, Nat Hurley, Robert Johnson, Vanessa Joosen, Jon Arno Lawson, Ebony Magnus, Michelle Martin, BFF Jennie Miskec, Amber Moore, Jennesia Pedri, Michelle Pidgeon, Phil Nel, Lissa Paul, Victoria Ford Smith, Suzanne Smythe, Björn Sundmark, Emma-Louise Silva, Victoria Thomas, Roberta Trites, and Cindy Xin. I'm especially grateful to the students at the Antwerp summer school who listened to early versions of the arguments in these pages, introduced me to new texts and international perspectives, and even attended a workshop in a pub when a fire forced us to evacuate our classroom.

Kenneth Kidd read and gave critical feedback on the prospectus that helped shape the contours of this project. Pete Kunze generously shared his expertise on Disney and animation and regularly sent me examples of childhood drinking in popular culture. Laura Mamo provided sharp insight and a close reading of the *E.T.* lesson. Anna Mae Duane encouraged me to embrace contradictions during intemperate conversations about temperance; her wit and smarts are soaked into these pages. My steadfast and brilliant collaborator Leigh Gilmore read every word of this book, including the endnotes, from its inception to its final draft; this book would not be what it is without her input.

I am grateful to the family and friends who supported me as I wrote, including Michael Meneer, Maisie Meneer, Terry Rogers, Rob Tierney, Chris Tierney, Dahra Zamudio, Brian Demuy, Marilyn Kwong, Lorraine and Rob Kitsos, Pavel Soukenik, Wendy and Ron Stuart, Jeff Hunter, Steph Weterings, and my parents, Tim and Mimi Marshall. This book is dedicated to the incomparable Angela Cummings alongside whom I learned the lessons of the drinking curriculum.

Notes

Introduction: Learning to Drink

1. *The Little Boy and His Mother* (Seth Bliss, 1833). Thank you to Laura Wasowicz, curator of children's literature at the American Antiquarian Society for locating and sharing this image.

2. For a history of adult fears about youth and the consumption of commercial culture, see Chapter 4 in Tom Engelhardt, *The End of Victory Culture: Cold War America and The Disillusioning of a Generation* (Amherst: University of Massachusetts Press, 2007). Additional context about the attempts of "drys" to limit alcohol and cigarette advertisements on television can be found in Pamela Pennock, "Televising Sin: Efforts to Restrict the Televised Advertisement of Cigarettes and Alcohol in the United States, 1950s to 1980s," *Historical Journal of Film, Radio and Television* 25, no. 4 (October 1, 2005): 619–36. Research on the representations of alcohol in children's materials gained traction throughout the new temperance movement of the 1970s and 1980s, most notably in the study *Television and Behavior, Ten Years of Scientific Progress and Implications for the Eighties* (Rockville: National Institute of Mental Health, 1982). Research that attempts to link representation to behavior is vast and typically comes out of the fields of communication, health, and education. A sample of such research includes Sonya Dal Cin et al., "Youth Exposure to Alcohol Use and Brand Appearances in Popular Contemporary Movies," *Addiction* 103, no. 12 (2008): 1925–32; Robert H. DuRant et al., "Tobacco and Alcohol Use Behaviors Portrayed in Music Videos: A Content Analysis," *American Journal of Public Health* 87, no. 7 (July 1997): 1131–35; Hugh Klein and Kenneth S. Shiffman, "Alcohol-Related Content of Animated Cartoons: A Historical Perspective," *Frontiers in Public Health* 1 (March 28, 2013): 1–11; Susan C. Hill et al., "Alcohol Advertisements in Youth-Oriented Magazines: Persuasive Themes and Responsibility Messages," *American Journal of Health*

Education 36, no. 5 (2005): 258–65; Mira Mayrhofer and Brigitte Naderer, "Mass Media as Alcohol Educator for Everyone? Effects of Portrayed Alcohol Consequences and the Influence of Viewers' Characteristics," *Media Psychology* 22, no. 2 (2019): 217–43; Cristel Antonia Russell et al., "Television's Cultivation of American Adolescents' Beliefs about Alcohol and the Moderating Role of Trait Reactance," *Journal of Children and Media* 8, no. 1 (January 1, 2014): 5–22; Erin L. Ryan and Keisha L. Hoerrner, "Let Your Conscience Be Your Guide: Smoking and Drinking in Disney's Animated Classics," *Mass Communication and Society* 7, no. 3 (July 1, 2004): 261–78.

3. Tara Parker-Pope, "Harry Potter and the Pint of Liquid Courage," *The New York Times*, 2009, D1; Trina Schart Hyman, *Little Red Riding Hood* (New York: Holiday House, 1983); "Little Red Riding Hood Banned," *Seattle Times*, May 19, 1990, https://archive.seattletimes.com/archive/?date=19900519&slug=1072598.

4. James R. Kincaid, *Erotic Innocence: The Culture of Child Molesting* (Durham: Duke University Press, 1998), 21.

5. Nicholas Mirzoeff, *How to See the World.* (London: Penguin Random House), 14.

6. Kincaid, *Erotic Innocence*, 19.

7. Centers for Disease Control and Prevention, "Underage Drinking," 2022, https://www.cdc.gov/alcohol/fact-sheets/underage-drinking.htm.

8. Kincaid, *Erotic Innocence*, 3.

9. Daniel Okrent, *Last Call: The Rise and Fall of Prohibition* (New York: Simon & Schuster, 2010), 7.

10. Andrew Barr, *Drink: A Social History of America* (New York: Carroll & Graf, 1999); Susan Cheever, *Drinking in America: Our Secret History* (New York: Hachette / Twelve, 2015); Okrent, *Last Call*. See also Mark Edward Lender and James Kirby Martin, *Drinking in America: A History* (New York: The Free Press, 1987) which, like Cheever's book, includes reference to drinking children.

11. Anne Higonnet, *Pictures of Innocence: The History and Crisis of Ideal Childhood* (London: Thames and Hudson, 1998), 14.

12. Timothy Cole, "'Old Enough to Live': Age, Alcohol, and Adulthood in the United States, 1970–1984," in *Age in America: The Colonial Era to the Present*, eds. Corinne T. Field and Nicholas L. Syrett (New York: New York University Press, 2015), 241.

13. For theorizations of age, see, for instance, Kathryn Bond Stockton, *The Queer Child, Or Growing Sideways in the Twentieth Century* (Durham: Duke University Press, 2009); Anna Mae Duane, *Suffering Childhood in Early America: Violence, Race, and the Making of the Child Victim* (Athens: University of Georgia Press, 2010); Nancy Lesko, *Act Your Age!: A Cultural Construction of Adolescence* (New York: Routledge, 2012); Robert Pogue Harrison, *Juvenescence: A Cultural History of Our Age* (Chicago: The University of Chicago Press, 2014); Sari Edelstein, *Adulthood and Other Fictions* (Oxford: Oxford University Press, 2018); and, Habiba Ibrahim,

Black Age: Oceanic Lifespans and the Time of Black Life (New York: New York University Press, 2021).

14. Joanna McClanahan, "20 Ways Toddlers are Just Like Your Drunk Friend, Scary Mommy, accessed November 20, 2022, https://www.scarymommy.com /toddlers-are-like-drunk-people; "Drunk Vs. Kid: Can YOU Guess Who Said this Crazy Quote?," video, 11:03, YouTube, posted by React, April 28, 2021, https://www .youtube.com/watch?v=ZN3fX34pvIA&ab_channel=REACT.

15. Jane Lilienfeld and Jeffrey Thomas Oxford, *The Languages of Addiction* (New York: St. Martin's Press, 1999). The link between drunkenness and bad behavior also arises in the nineteenth century, see Harry Gene Levine, "The Good Creature of God and Demon Rum: Colonial American and 19th Century Ideas about Alcohol, Crime and Accidents," in *Alcohol and Disinhibition: Nature and Meaning of the Link*, eds. Robin Room and Gary Collins (Rockville: U.S. Department of Health and Human Services, 1983), 111–61.

16. *The Glass of Whisky* (Philadelphia: The American Sunday School Union, 1860), 5–6.

17. Paul E. Reckner and Stephen A. Brighton, "'Free from All Vicious Habits': Archaeological Perspectives on Class Conflict and the Rhetoric of Temperance," *Historical Archaeology* 33, no. 1 (1999): 67. See also Lisa McGirr, *The War on Alcohol: Prohibition and the Rise of the American State* (New York: W. W. Norton & Co., 2016). The link between antisemitism and Prohibition as an outgrowth of anti-immigrant sentiment as well as evidence of different norms around childhood drinking is taken up in Marni Davis, *Jews and Booze: Becoming American in the Age of Prohibition* (New York: New York University Press, 2012).

18. Reckner and Brighton, "'Free from All," 64.

19. Nyholm's *Las Palmas* was an instant hit when the trailer circulated on YouTube, garnering more than 20 million views. It was selected for Sundance in 2012. For more, see http://en-us.laspalmasmovie.com/.

20. Noël Carroll, "Horror and Humor," *Journal of Aesthetics and Art Criticism* 57, no. 2 (1999): 152.

21. Lance Morrow, "Wondering If Children Are Necessary," *Time* 113, no. 10 (1979): 42.

22. According to the *OED*, the term misopaedia, a hatred or dislike of children, was first used in 1890. For more on violence in children's literature and culture, see Maria Tatar, *Off With Their Heads!: Fairy Tales and the Culture of Childhood* (Princeton: Princeton University Press, 1992); Elizabeth Marshall, *Graphic Girlhoods: Visualizing Education and Violence* (New York: Routledge, 2018); Eric L. Tribunella, "Pedophobia and the Orphan Girl in *Pollyanna* and *A Series of Unfortunate Events*," in *Gender(ed) Identities: Critical Rereadings of Gender in Children's and Young Adult Literature*, eds. Tricia Clasen and Holly Hassel (New York: Routledge, 2016), 136–49; Karen Coats, "Child-Hating: *Peter Pan* in the Context of Victorian Hatred," in *J.M. Barrie's Peter Pan In and Out of Time: A Children's Classic at 100* (Lanham: Scarecrow Press, 2006), 3–22. The related term

ephebiphobia, a fear of teenagers, was coined by Kirk A. Astroth, "Beyond Ephebiphobia: Problem Adults or Problem Youths?," *The Phi Delta Kappan* 75, no. 5 (August 26, 1994): 411–13.

23. Alan Dundes, "The Dead Baby Joke Cycle," *Western Folklore* 38, no. 3 (1979): 145.

24. Morrow, "Wondering If Children," 43.

25. Stephen Schiff, "Edward Gorey and the Tao of Nonsense," *The New Yorker*, 1992, 88.

26. Ibid.

27. Duane, *Suffering Childhood*, 3.

28. Peter McGraw and Joel Warner, *The Humor Code: A Global Search for What Makes Things Funny* (New York: Simon & Schuster, 2014), 120.

29. Tom Tomlinson, "Uncomfortable Humor," *The Hastings Center Report* 42, no. 3 (August 19, 2012): 9.

30. *The Simpsons*, Season 8, episode 18, "Homer vs. the Eighteenth Amendment," directed by Bob Anderson, written by Matt Groening, James L. Brooks, and Sam Simon, aired on March 16, 1997, on Fox Network.

31. Kevin Glynn, "Bartmania: The Social Reception of an Unruly Image," *Camera Obscura: Feminism, Culture, and Media Studies*, 13, no. 2 (July 1996): 61.

32. Hillary Chute, *Graphic Women: Life Narrative and Contemporary Comics* (New York: Columbia University Press, 2010); Hillary Chute, *Why Comics? From Underground to Everywhere* (New York: Harper Collins, 2017).

33. Steven Spielberg, *E.T. the Extra-Terrestrial* (U.S.A.: Universal Pictures, 1982).

34. Mary Hambly, "An Interview with Lynda Barry," in *Backbone 4: Humor by Northwest Women* (Seattle: Seal Press, 1982), 26.

Lesson One: D is for Drunkard

1. Harry Gene Levine, "The Alcohol Problem in America: From Temperance to Alcoholism," *British Journal of Addiction* 79, no. 1 (1984): 110.

2. Susan Cheever, *Drinking in America: Our Secret History* (New York: Hachette/Twelve, 2015), 92; 7.

3. For more on childhood drinking in the United States see, Mark Edward Lender and James Kirby Martin, *Drinking in America: A History* (New York: The Free Press, 1982).

4. Albert Barnes, *The Immorality of The Traffic in Ardent Spirits: A Discourse* (Philadelphia: George, Latimer & Co., 1834), 30. Drinking in the United States hit "a peak of 7.1 gallons of pure alcohol per person per year in 1830," Emma Green "Colonial Americans Drank Roughly Three Times as Much as Americans Do Now," *The Atlantic*, June 29, 2015, https://www.theatlantic.com/health/archive/2015/06/benjamin-rush-booze-morality-democracy/396818/. For a history of drinking habits in the United States, see W. J. Rorabaugh, *The Alcoholic Republic: An American Tradition* (New York & Oxford: Oxford University Press, 1979).

5. Benjamin Rush, *An Inquiry Into the Effects of Ardent Spirits Upon the Human Body and Mind: With An Account of the Means of Preventing, and of the Remedies For Curing Them* (New York: Cornelius Davis, 1785).

6. Megan Gambino, "This Chart from 1790 Lays Out the Many Dangers of Alcoholism," *Smithsonian*, March 27, 2015, https://www.smithsonianmag.com /history/chart-1790-lays-out-many-dangers-alcoholism-180954777.

7. William L. White, "Addiction Medicine in America: Its Birth and Early History (1750–1935) with a Modern Postscript," in *Principles of Addiction Medicine*, eds. Richard Ries, et al. (Philadelphia: Wolters Kluwer, 2009), 327.

8. Holly Berkley Fletcher, *Gender and the American Temperance Movement of the Nineteenth Century* (New York: Routledge, 2008), 5. See also, Joseph R. Gusfield, *Symbolic Crusade: Status Politics and the American Temperance Movement*, 2nd ed. (Urbana and Chicago: University of Illinois Press, 1986).

9. Mark Lawrence Schrad, "The Forgotten History of Black Prohibitionism," *Politico*, February 6, 2021, https://www.politico.com/news/magazine/2021/02/06 /forgotten-black-history-prohibition-temperance-movement-461215.

10. Nazera Sadiq Wright, "'Our Hope Is in the Rising Generation': Locating African American Children's Literature in the Children's Department of the *Colored American*," in *Who Writes for Black Children?*, eds. Katharine Capshaw and Anna Mae Duane (Minneapolis: University of Minnesota Press, 2017), 147–63

11. Colin Marshall, "The First Children's Picture Book, 1658's *Orbis Sensualium Pictus*," *Open Culture*, May 22, 2014, http://www.openculture.com/2014/05/first -childrens-picture-book-1658s-orbis-sensualium-pictus.html. For more on the educational importance of Comenius in a U.S. context, see Patricia Crain, *The Story of A: The Alphabetization of America from The New England Primer to The Scarlet Letter* (Stanford: Stanford University Press, 2000), 26–38. Comenius' legacy is evident in the National Council of Teachers of English *Orbis Pictus* award for nonfiction given out each year.

12. Johann Amos Comenius, *Orbis Sensualium Pictus* (New York: T. & J. Swords, 1810), 160.

13. Joseph R. Gusfield, *The Culture of Public Problems: Drinking-Driving and the Symbolic Order* (Chicago: The University of Chicago Press, 1981), 150.

14. Marty Roth, *Drunk the Night Before: An Anatomy of Intoxication* (Minneapolis: University of Minnesota Press, 2005), xiii.

15. Karen Sánchez-Eppler, "Temperance in the Bed of a Child: Incest and Social Order in Nineteenth-Century America," *American Quarterly* 47, no. 1 (1995): 6.

16. *A Was an Archer, or A New Amusing Alphabet For Children* (Newark: Benjamin Olds, 1836). For more on the history of alphabet books in the United States, consult Crain, *The Story of A*.

17. Charles Wakely, "The Education of Children in Temperance Principles," in *CP 1890*, 125, c.f., Johan Edman, "Temperance and Modernity: Alcohol Consumption as a Collective Problem, 1885–1913," *Journal of Social History* 49, no. 1 (September 11, 2015): 29.

18. Charles Jewett, *Temperance Toy* (Boston: Whipple and Damrell, 1840).

19. Grant Paton-Simpson, "The Varied Meanings of Drinking and Intoxication—A Review," *Contemporary Drug Problems* 23 (1996): 223. See also, Craig MacAndrew and Robert B. Edgerton, *Drunken Comportment: A Social Explanation* (Chicago: Aldine Publishing Company, 1969); and, Mary Douglas, *Constructive Drinking: Perspectives from Anthropology* (New York: Routledge, 1987).

20. Jewett, *Temperance Toy*, 6.

21. Charles Jewett, *The Youth's Temperance Lecturer* (Boston: Whipple and Damrell, 1841), 11.

22. Ibid., 5.

23. William Gleason, "Ten Nights in a Bar-Room and the Visual Culture of Temperance," in *Must Read: Rediscovering American Bestsellers From Charlotte Temple to The Da Vinci Code*, eds. Sarah Churchwell and Thomas Ruys Smith (New York: Bloomsbury Publishing, 2012), 102. On using visual culture to teach children temperance principles in the UK, see Annemarie McAllister, "Picturing the Demon Drink: How Children Were Shown Temperance Principles in the Band of Hope," *Visual Resources* 28, no. 4 (2012): 309–23.

24. The redrawn images by Pilliner that adapted Cruikshank's originals can be viewed at http://utc.iath.virginia.edu/sentimnt/galltsaaf.html. For more on the road-to-ruin script, see Frank Murray, "Picturing the 'Road to Ruin': Visual Representations of a Standard Temperance Narrative, 1830–1855," *Visual Resources* 28, no. 4 (2012): 290–308.

25. Trevor Jackson, "Demon Drink: George Cruikshank's 'The Worship of Bacchus' in Focus," *British Medical Journal* 322 (2001): 1495. Cruikshank's anti-alcohol sentiments found their way into his work for children, specifically, *George Cruikshank's Fairy Library* (London: George Bell and Sons, 1865). See Charles Dickens, "Frauds on the Fairies," in *Fantastic Literature: A Critical Reader*, ed. David Sandner (Westport, CT & London: Praeger, 2004), 56–58 for a critique of temperance discourse in Cruikshank's *Fairy Library*.

26. Timothy Shay Arthur, *Grappling with the Monster; Or, The Curse and the Cure of Strong Drink* (New York: J. W. Lovell, 1877). Arthur was also the author of the nineteenth century's best-selling temperance narrative *Ten Nights in a Bar-Room and What I Saw There* (Philadelphia: J. W. Bradley, 1854).

27. Viviana A. Zelizer, "The Price and Value of Children: The Case of Children's Insurance," *American Journal of Sociology* 86, no. 5 (1981): 1036–56; Karin Calvert, *Children in the House: The Material Culture of Early Childhood, 1600–1900* (Northeastern University Press, 1992); Anne Higonnet, *Pictures of Innocence: The History and Crisis of Ideal Childhood* (London: Thames and Hudson, 1998); Erika Langmuir, *Imagining Childhood* (New Haven & London: Yale University Press, 2006); Anna Mae Duane, *Suffering Childhood in Early America: Violence, Race, and the Making of the Child Victim* (Athens: University of Georgia Press, 2010); Robin Bernstein, *Racial Innocence: Performing American Childhood from Slavery to Civil Rights* (New York: New York University Press, 2011).

28. Susan Zieger, *Inventing the Addict: Drugs, Race, and Sexuality in Nineteenth-Century British and American Literature* (Amherst: University of Massachusetts Press, 2008), 199.

29. Elaine Frantz Parsons, *Manhood Lost: Fallen Drunkards and Redeeming Women in the Nineteenth-Century United States* (Baltimore: Johns Hopkins University Press, 2003), 186.

30. Roth, *Drunk the Night Before*, xiii.

31. Ibid., 155. Eve Kosofsky Sedgwick theorizes the pathologizing of the drug user as "addict" in the nineteenth century in her chapter "Epidemics of the Will" in *Tendencies* (Durham: Duke University Press, 1993).

32. Duane, *Suffering Childhood*, 3. Much has been written about the political use of the wounded child, including Patricia Holland, *What Is a Child? Popular Images of Childhood* (Virago, 1992); Leigh Gilmore and Elizabeth Marshall, "Girls in Crisis: Rescue and Transnational Feminist Autobiographical Resistance," *Feminist Studies* 36, no. 3 (2010): 667–90; Wendy Hesford, *Spectacular Rhetorics: Human Rights Visions, Recognitions, Feminisms* (Durham: Duke University Press, 2011); Leigh Gilmore and Elizabeth Marshall, *Witnessing Girlhood: Toward a Tradition of Intersectional Life Writing* (New York: Fordham University Press, 2019). For an analysis of the vulnerable child in anti-alcohol campaigns, see Helena Goscilo, "From Double-Voiced to Univocal: Devious, Desirous, and Declarative Childhoods in Soviet Posters," in *Historical and Cultural Transformations of Russian Childhood: Myths and Realities*, eds. Marina Balina, Larissa Rudova, and Antastasia Kostetskaya (New York: Routledge, 2022): 79–118.

33. See, for instance, Sánchez-Eppler, "Temperance in the Bed."

34. Jewett, *The Youth's Temperance Lecturer*, 20.

35. Ibid. In the 1861 edition of the book the father is referred to as an "intoxicated man."

36. Maria Tatar, *Off With Their Heads!: Fairy Tales and the Culture of Childhood* (Princeton: Princeton University Press, 1992), 31.

37. Karen Halttunen, "Humanitarianism and the Pornography of Pain in Anglo-American Culture, *The American Historical Review* 100, no. 2 (1995): 325.

38. Norton Mezvinsky, "Scientific Temperance Instruction in the Schools," *History of Education Quarterly* 1, no. 1 (1961): 54. For an in-depth history of WCTU and Scientific Temperance in schools see Jonathan Zimmerman, "'The Queen of the Lobby': Mary Hunt, Scientific Temperance, and the Dilemma of Democratic Education in America, 1879–1906," *History of Education Quarterly* 32, no. 1 (1992): 1–30; Jonathan Zimmerman, "The Dilemma of Miss Jolly: Scientific Temperance and Teacher Professionalism, 1882–1904," *History of Education Quarterly* 34, no. 4 (1994): 413–31; Jonathan Zimmerman, *Distilling Democracy: Alcohol Education in America's Public Schools, 1880–1925* (Lawrence: University of Kansas Press, 1999).

39. Julia Colman, *Alcohol and Hygiene: An Elementary Lesson Book for Schools* (New York: National Temperance Society, 1887).

40. Richard David Mosier, *Making the American Mind: Social and Moral Ideas in the McGuffey Readers* (New York: Russell & Russell, 1965).

41. Philip McGowan, "AA and the Redeployment of Temperance Literature," *Journal of American Studies* 48, no. 1 (2014): 78.

42. Addiction and recovery themes are also present in children's literary fiction. See, for example, Sarah Wadsworth, "'When the Cup Has Been Drained': Addiction and Recovery in *The Wind in the Willows*," *Children's Literature* 42 (2014): 42–70. For a consideration of how children of alcoholics are represented in children's literature, consult Meagan Lacy, "Portraits of Children of Alcoholics: Stories That Add Hope to Hope," *Children's Literature in Education* 46, no. 4 (2015): 343–58.

43. LeClair Bissell and Richard Watherwax, *The Cat Who Drank Too Much* (Bantam, CT: Bibulophile Press, 1982). Dr. Bissell created the Smithers Alcoholism Treatment and Training Center at Roosevelt Hospital in New York, the first university-affiliated, hospital-based alcohol rehabilitation unit in the United States. She received the Elizabeth Blackwell Award of the American Medical Women's Association and the Marty Mann Medal of the National Council on Alcoholism. For an interview with LeClair Bissell, see William L. White, "Reflections of an Addiction Treatment Pioneer: An Interview with LeClair Bissell, MD (1928–2008)," William White Papers, 1997, chestnut.org/resources/994201fd-3ff3-487c-8fb6 -afaeaa0ee00a/2011-Dr.-LeClair-Bissell-1997-v2.pdf.

44. Fanny Britt, *Louis Undercover*, Illus., Isabelle Arsenault (Toronto: Groundwood Books, 2017). The graphic novel won the Association for Library Service to Children Notable Children's Book, Bank Street College of Education Best Children's Books of the Year, and *School Library Journal* Top 10 Graphic Novels of 2017. It also received starred reviews in *Publisher's Weekly*, *School Library Journal*, *Booklist*, and *The Bulletin of the Center for Children's Books*.

45. Britt, *Louis Undercover*, 15.

46. Ibid., 132.

47. See Breitenbach, "Sons of the Fathers: Temperance Reformers and the Legacy of the American Revolution," *Journal of the Early Republic*, 3, no. 1 (1983): 69–82.

48. Gabrielle Glaser, *Her Best-Kept Secret: Why Women Drink and How They Can Regain Control* (New York: Simon & Schuster, 2013), 97.

49. Dan Munro, "Inside The $35 Billion Addiction Treatment Industry," *Forbes*, April 27, 2015, https://www.forbes.com/sites/danmunro/2015/04/27/inside-the-35 -billion-addiction-treatment-industry/#138f111117dc.

50. Paton-Simpson, "The Varied Meanings," 223.

Lesson Two: No Pets, No Drunks, No Children

1. *The Tampa Tribune*, March 15, 1951, 34.

2. Alfred Gordon, "A Study of Fourteen Cases of Alcoholism in Children Apparently Free from Morbid Heredity," *Medical Record*, 1913, 433.

3. Peter C. Kunze, "Stay Tuned: A Political History of Saturday Morning Cartoons," in *A Companion to Children's Literature*, eds. Karen Coats, Deborah Stevenson, and Vivian Yenika-Agbaw (Wiley, 2022), 106; 109.

4. Pamela Pennock, "Televising Sin: Efforts to Restrict the Televised Advertisement of Cigarettes and Alcohol in the United States, 1950s to 1980s," *Historical Journal of Film, Radio and Television* 25, no. 4 (October 1, 2005): 619–36.

5. Muriel Andrin, "Back to the 'Slap': Slapstick's Hyperbolic Gesture and the Rhetoric of Violence," in *Slapstick Comedy*, eds. Tom Paulus and Rob King (New York: Routledge, 2010), 226.

6. Edward Slingerland, *Drunk: How We Sipped, Danced, and Stumbled Our Way to Civilization* (New York: Little, Brown Spark, 2021), 290.

7. Sarah Baird, "The Boozy Underbelly of Saturday Morning Cartoons," *Eater*, August 10, 2015, https://www.eater.com/drinks/2015/8/10/9126181/alcohol-and-cartoons.

8. Thomas Lamarre, "Speciesism, Part III: Neoteny and the Politics of Life," *Mechademia* 6, no. 1 (2011): 113.

9. Walter Benjamin, "On Mickey Mouse," in *A Mickey Mouse Reader*, ed. Garry Apgar (Jackson: University Press of Mississippi, 2014), 20.

10. Norman M. Klein, *Seven Minutes: The Life and Death of the American Animated Cartoon* (New York: Verson, 1994), 70.

11. Andrin, "Back to the 'Slap,'" 229.

12. Garry Apgar, "Introduction," in *A Mickey Mouse Reader*, ed. Garry Apgar (Jackson: University Press of Mississippi, 2014), xvii–xxi.

13. Nicholas Sammond, *Babes in Tomorrowland: Walt Disney and the Making of the American Child, 1930–1960* (Durham: Duke University Press, 2005), 167.

14. For a reading of this short as a critique of urban life in the U.S., see Keri Fredericks, "*The Country Cousin*: Advocating an Arcadian America," *Athanor* 26 (2008): 81–89. See the chapter entitled "A Drunken Mouse" in Jake S. Friedman, *The Disney Revolt: The Great Labor War of Animation's Golden Age* (Chicago: Chicago Review Press, 2022) for background on the creation of the animated drinking scene. Heavy drinking was an "occupational hazard" for Disney animators; see Neal Gabler, *Walt Disney: The Triumph of the American Imagination* (New York: Vintage Books, 2006), 239.

15. Nicholas Sammond, *Birth of an Industry: Blackface Minstrelsy and the Rise of American Animation* (Durham: Duke University Press, 2015), 203.

16. Anna Mae Duane, *Suffering Childhood in Early America: Violence, Race, and the Making of the Child Victim* (Athens: University of Georgia Press, 2010), 5.

17. Benjamin Ivry, "The Secret Jewish History Of 'Dumbo,'" *Forward*, April 4, 2019, https://forward.com/culture/film-tv/422025/the-secret-jewish-history-of-dumbo/.

18. Jennifer Hunter, "Jumbo the Elephant: From Child Star to Boozed-up Wreck," *Toronto Star*, March 7, 2014, https://www.thestar.com/news/insight/2014/03/07/jumbo_the_elephant_from_child_star_to_boozedup_wreck.html. See also, John Sutherland, *Jumbo: The Unauthorised Biography of a Victorian Sensation*

(London: Aurum Press, 2014). The elephant tragically died in 1885 after being hit by a train while on tour in Ontario, Canada.

19. The animated drunken adventure of Abner provided a template for Timothy Q. Mouse; see Fredericks, *"The Country Cousin,"* 81.

20. Peter Jensen Brown, "The Colorful History and Etymology of 'Pink Elephant,'" *Early Sports and Pop Culture*, August 20, 2014, https://esnpc.blogspot .com/2014/08/the-colorful-history-and-etymology-of.html.

21. The term, *delirium tremens*, and its hallucinations appear as early as 1822. See, Stephen Brown, "Observations on Delirium Tremens, or the Delirium of Drunkards, with Cases," *The American Medical Recorder of Original Papers and Intelligence in Medicine and Surgery*, 5, no. 2 (April, 1822): 194.

22. For a discussion of the scene in terms of form, style, and disparate animation styles at work in the Disney studio at the time, see Mark Langer, "Regionalism in Disney Animation: Pink Elephants and Dumbo," *Film History* 4, no. 4 (October 7, 1990): 305–21.

23. Klein, *Seven Minutes*, 71.

24. The song was composed by Oliver Wallace and Ned Washington

25. Nicholas Sammond, "Dumbo, Disney, and Difference: Walt Disney Productions and Film as Children's Literature," eds. Lynne Vallone and Julia Mickenberg, *The Oxford Handbook of Children's Literature* (Oxford: Oxford University Press, 2011), 156.

26. Sammond, *Birth of an Industry*, 256.

27. Nicola Shulman, "The Ears Have It," *The Times Literary Supplement*, no. 6058 (May 10, 2019): 20.

28. Bosley Crowther, "Walt Disney's Cartoon, 'Dumbo,' a Fanciful Delight, Opens at the Broadway," *The New York Times*, October 24, 1941, 27.

29. Esther Leslie, *Hollywood Flatlands: Animation, Critical Theory and The Avant-Garde* (London: Verso, 2001), 30.

30. Practical Folks. *"Dumbo* (Drunk Disney #4)," YouTube Video, 12:58, February 5, 2014, https://www.youtube.com/watch?v=TUbialwfMzs. Tim Burton's 2019 live-action remake of the film edits out the champagne-infused adventure even as the script written by Ehren Kruger winks at the drunken antics of the original. In Burton's version, Dumbo watches sober pink elephants as part of the circus show. When a clown runs into the tent with a bottle in hand and says, "champagne for Dumbo," the ringmaster shoos him away, stating "no booze near the baby."

31. "Public vs. Private Persona," *PBS*, 0:06, August 29, 2017, https://www.pbs.org /wgbh/americanexperience/features/public-vs-private-persona/. See also, Gabler, *Walt Disney*, 513.

32. Erin L. Ryan and Keisha L. Hoerrner, "Let Your Conscience Be Your Guide: Smoking and Drinking in Disney's Animated Classics," *Mass Communication and Society* 7, no. 3 (July 1, 2004): 261. See also, Hugh Klein and Kenneth S. Shiffman, "Alcohol-Related Content of Animated Cartoons: A Historical Perspective," *Frontiers in Public Health* 1 (March 28, 2013): 1–11.

33. https://cartoonresearch.com/index.php/holy-matrimony-a-stack-of-storks-part-2/.

34. There is one exception in the 1955 short "Pappy's Puppy" when a sober Drunk Stork delivers the baby to the right house.

35. Morwenna Griffiths and Michael A. Peters, "'I Knew Jean-Paul Sartre': Philosophy of Education as Comedy," *Educational Philosophy and Theory* 46, no. 2 (2014): 139.

36. *Tiny Toons*, Season 2, episode 3, "Elephant Issues (Why Dizzy Can't Read / C.L.I.D.E. and Prejudice / One Beer," directed by Ken Boyer, aired September 18, 1991 on Fox, https://www.imdb.com/title/tt0394957/.

37. Banned from first run syndication on Fox in 1995, the episode was re-released on DVD in *Volume 3: Crazy Crew Rescues* in 2013. See, Richard Milner, "The Tiny Toons Episode that Caused an Outrage," *Grunge*, September 28, 2020, https://www .grunge.com/253089/the-tiny-toons-episode-that-caused-an-outrage/.

38. Roger Cormier, "15 Looney Facts About 'Tiny Toon Adventures,'" *Mental Floss*, April 18, 2016, https://www.mentalfloss.com/article/64341/15-looney-facts-about-tiny -toon-adventures.

39. During the 1980s advocates of the new temperance movement, such as Project SMART (Stop Marketing Alcohol on Radio and Television), pressured congress to restrict the marketing of alcohol in the U.S. For more, see Pennock, "Televising Sin," 628.

Lesson Three: "Friends Don't Let Friends Drink and Drive"

1. Steven Spielberg and Melissa Mathison, *E.T. the Extra-Terrestrial: From Concept to Classic* (New York: Newmarket Press, 2012), 86.

2. Steven Spielberg, *E.T. the Extra-Terrestrial* (U.S.A.: Universal Pictures, 1982); David Sterritt, "Two More Films From Spielberg, A One-Man Fantasy Factory," *The Christian Science Monitor*, 1982, 19; Aljean Harmetz, "'E.T.' Grosses $13 Million For Opening Weekend," *The New York Times*, June 15, 1982, C10; "'E.T.' Scores A Box Office Record," *Associated Press*, July 7, 1982.

3. Robin Wood, "E.T.—The Extraterrestrial," in *International Dictionary of Films and Filmmakers*, eds. Sara Pendergast and Tom Pendergast, 4th ed., vol. 1 (Detroit: St. James Press, 2000), 393.

4. "ET: An Extraordinary Extra-Terrestrial," *Associated Press*, July 24, 1982.

5. Vincent Canby, "Film View: Exploring Inner and Outer Space With Steven Spielberg," *The New York Times*, June 13, 1982, 29.

6. Vincent Canby, "'E.T.,' Fantasy From Spielberg," *The New York Times*, June 11, 1982, C14.

7. Sara Willott and Antonia C. Lyons, "Consuming Male Identities: Masculinities, Gender Relations and Alcohol Consumption in Aotearoa New Zealand," *Journal of Community & Applied Social Psychology* 22, no. 4 (2012): 330–45; Lois A. West, "Negotiating Masculinities in American Drinking Subcultures," *The Journal of Men's Studies* 9, no. 3 (June 1, 2001): 371–92; Geoffrey Hunt and Tamar Antin,

"Gender and Intoxication: From Masculinity to Intersectionality," *Drugs: Education, Prevention and Policy* 26, no. 1 (2019): 70–78.

8. Edward Slingerland, *Drunk: How We Sipped, Danced, and Stumbled Our Way to Civilization* (New York: Little, Brown Spark, 2021), 11.

9. L. Frank Baum, *The Annotated Wizard of Oz*, ed. Michael Patrick Hearn (New York: W. W. Norton, 2000), 283.

10. Joel W. Grube, "Alcohol in the Media: Drinking Portrayals, Alcohol Advertising, and Alcohol Consumption Among Youth," in *Reducing Underage Drinking: A Collective Responsibility*, eds. Richard J. Bonnie and Mary Ellen O'Connell (Washington, D.C.: National Academies Press, 2004), 602. See also, Adam O Goldstein et al., "Tobacco and Alcohol Use in G-Rated Children's Animated Films," *JAMA* 281, no. 12 (1999): 1131–36.

11. Sterritt, "Two More Films," 19.

12. Jay Scott, "E.T. A Cheery Children's Crusade," *Globe and Mail*, May 27, 1982, 21.

13. "ET: An Extraordinary Extra-Terrestrial."

14. Canby, "Film View," 29.

15. Anna Green, "Why Do We Laugh When We're Scared?," *Mental Floss*, October 16, 2015, https://www.mentalfloss.com/article/69830/why-do-we-laugh-when -were-scared.

16. For an analysis of the identification of the child with the "freak" in *E.T.*, see Lori Merish, "Cuteness and Commodity Aesthetics: Tom Thumb and Shirley Temple," in *Freakery: Cultural Spectacles of the Extraordinary Body*, ed. Rosemarie Garland-Thomson (New York: New York University Press, 1996), 189.

17. Neil Postman, *The Disappearance of Childhood* (New York: Random House, 1982); Julia Mickenberg and Lynne Vallone, "Introduction," in *The Oxford Handbook of Children's Literature*, eds. Julia Mickenberg and Lynne Vallone (Oxford: Oxford University Press, 2011), 16. See also, Douglas Kellner, "Poltergeists, Gender, and Class in the Age of Reagan and Bush," in *Hidden Foundation: Cinema and the Question of Class*, eds. David E. James and Rick Berg (Minneapolis: University of Minnesota Press, 1996), 217–39.

18. Intoxicated Drivers was the first anti-drunk driving organization in the U.S., started in 1978 by Doris Aiken. Students Against Drunk Driving (S.A.D.D.) was established in 1981. For detailed discussion of the rise of Mothers against Drunk Drivers, see Craig Reinarman, "The Social Construction of an Alcohol Problem: The Case of Mothers against Drunk Drivers and Social Control in the 1980s," *Theory and Society* 17, no. 1 (1988): 91–120.

19. Busch was back in jail again in 1985 for felony drunk driving. See, "Catalyst for MADD Arrested Again: Drunk Driver Served 9 Months in Fatal 1980 Accident," *Los Angeles Times*, April 19, 1985, https://www.latimes.com/archives/la-xpm-1985-04 -19-mn-14951-story.html.

20. For the history of drunk driving in the U.S., see Joseph R. Gusfield, *The Culture of Public Problems: Drinking-Driving and the Symbolic Order* (Chicago:

The University of Chicago Press, 1981); Barron H. Lerner, *One for the Road: Drunk Driving Since 1900* (Baltimore: Johns Hopkins University Press, 2011).

21. "Advertisement: Drunk Driving Dept.," *Good Housekeeping* 183, no. 2 (August 1976): 163. Disney's 1979 animated educational film aimed at youth *Understanding Alcohol Use and Abuse* (one of the films sponsored by the Upjohn pharmaceutical company) includes a segment on drunk driving that explained the physiological effects of drinking, the four stages of inebriation, and how alcohol disrupted the balance between emotion and reason. The main character was a middle-aged white man and the only person harmed in the film is the driver.

22. Timothy Cole, "'Old Enough to Live': Age, Alcohol, and Adulthood in the United States, 1970–1984," in *Age in America: The Colonial Era to the Present*, eds. Corinne T. Field and Nicholas L. Syrett (New York: New York University Press, 2015), 241.

23. Traci L. Toomey, Toben F. Nelson, and Kathleen M. Lenk, "The Age-21 Minimum Legal Drinking Age: A Case Study Linking Past and Current Debates," *Addiction* 104, no. 12 (December 2009), 1958. Additionally, see Henry Wechsler, ed., *Minimum-Drinking-Age Laws: An Evaluation* (Lexington: Lexington Books, 1980).

24. Jenna Birch, "Why the Drinking Age Is 21 in the United States," *Teen Vogue*, July 17, 2016, https://www.teenvogue.com/story/minimum-drinking-age-legal-21 -america-history.

25. Clifford Berman, "Is *Your* Child a Secret Alcoholic?," *Good Housekeeping* 192, no. 6 (June 1981): 215.

26. C. Louis Bassano, "Of Adolescents and Alcohol," *The New York Times*, April 18, 1982.

27. James Barron, "The Teen Drug of Choice: Alcohol," *The New York Times*, August 7, 1988.

28. COTY, "When Will Teens Sober Up?," *Seventeen*, 42, no. 11 (1983): 75.

29. Ibid.

30. Laura Dreuth Zeman, "Mothers Against Drunk Driving: How Two Mothers' Personal Pain Birthed a Social Movement," in *The 21st Century Motherhood Movement: Mothers Speak Out on Why We Need to Change the World and How to Do It*, ed. Andrea O'Reilly (Branford: Demeter Press, 2011), 700.

31. Michael Jackson was personally thanked by then-President Ronald Reagan at a White House ceremony in 1985 for donating his Grammy-award-winning song "Beat It" for use in the "Skeletons" television and radio PSAs.

32. "Presidential Commission on Drunk Driving: Final Report" (Washington, D.C.: Presidential Commission on Drunk Driving, 1983), 11.

33. Ted Galen Carpenter, "The New Anti-Youth Movement," *The Nation* 240, no. 2 (January 19, 1985): 39.

34. Ibid., 39.

35. Joseph R. Gusfield, *Contested Meanings: The Construction of Alcohol Problems* (Madison: University of Wisconsin Press), 90.

36. S. Georgia Nugent, "Raising the Drinking Age to 21 Has Been a Disastrous 30-Year Experiment," *The New York Times*, February 15, 2015, https://www.nytimes.com/roomfordebate/2015/02/10/you-must-be-21-to-drink/raising-the-drinking-age-to-21-has-been-a-disasterous-30-year-experiment. The Drinking Age Act remains a point of contention, see Camille Paglia, "It's Time to Let Teenagers Drink Again," *Time* 183, no. 19 (May 19, 2014): 22.; Gabrielle Glaser, "Return the Drinking Age to 18, and Enforce It," *The New York Times*, February 10, 2015, https://www.nytimes.com/roomfordebate/2015/02/10/you-must-be-21-to-drink/return-the-drinking-age-to-18-and-enforce-it.

37. The filmmakers initially asked Mars Inc. to put M&M's in the film for the now iconic scene in which Elliott leads a trail of treats out for the alien, but the company declined. For more on the history of brand placement in film and *E.T.*'s legacy, see Jay Newell, Charles T. Salmon, and Susan Chang, "The Hidden History of Product Placement," *Journal of Broadcasting & Electronic Media* 50, no. 4 (2006): 575–94; Katy Kroll, "The Most Egregious Product Placements in Movie & TV History," *Rolling Stone*, June 4, 2013, https://www.rollingstone.com/movies/movie-lists/the-most-egregious-product-placements-in-movie-tv-history-10988/e-t-the-extra-terrestrial-20525/.

38. Janet Maslin, "Plugging Products in Movies as an Applied Art," *The New York Times*, November 15, 1982, C11. Product placement to advertise alcohol remains a common approach to marketing, see Ben Panko, "From Budweiser to Heineken, Alcohol Brands Are Rampant in Hollywood Films," *Smithsonian*, May 9, 2017, https://www.smithsonianmag.com/science-nature/budweiser-heineken-alcohol-brands-are-now-rampant-hollywood-films-180963207/. Alcohol companies also have a history of direct advertising to youth, Susan C. Hill et al., "Alcohol Advertisements in Youth-Oriented Magazines: Persuasive Themes and Responsibility Messages," *American Journal of Health Education* 36, no. 5 (2005): 258–65; Joel W. Grube, "Alcohol in the Media: Drinking Portrayals, Alcohol Advertising, and Alcohol Consumption Among Youth"; Joel W. Grube and Lawrence Wallack, "Television Beer Advertising and Drinking Knowledge, Beliefs, and Intentions among Schoolchildren," *American Journal of Public Health* 84, no. 2 (February 1994): 254–59; Paul J. Chung et al., "Association Between Adolescent Viewership and Alcohol Advertising on Cable Television.," *American Journal of Public Health* 100, no. 3 (March 2010): 555–62. Alcohol brands are also advertised on social media outlets like Instagram, see Adam E. Barry et al., "Alcohol Advertising on Social Media: Examining the Content of Popular Alcohol Brands on Instagram," *Substance Use & Misuse* 53, no. 14 (2018): 2413–20. Humor is often a tactic in alcohol advertising, see Simone Pettigrew et al., "Get Them Laughing to Get Them Drinking: An Analysis of Alcohol Advertising Themes Across Multiple Media in Australia," *Journal of Studies on Alcohol and Drugs* 81, no. 3 (May 1, 2020): 311–19.

39. For more, see B. Erin Cole and Allyson Brantley, "The Coors Boycott: When a Beer Can Signaled Your Politics," *Colorado Public Radio*, October 3, 2014, https://www.cpr.org/2014/10/03/the-coors-boycott-when-a-beer-can-signaled-your-politics/.

40. Grace Lichtenstein, "Rocky Mountain High," *The New York Times Magazine*, 1975, 14. Because the beer wasn't licensed to sell east of the Mississippi, Coors was considered rare.

41. Barron H. Lerner, "How Americans Learned to Condemn Drunk Driving," *What It Means to Be American*, January 17, 2019, https://www.whatit meanstobeamerican.org/identities/how-americans-learned-to-condemn-drunk -driving/.

42. Lightner was not a teetotaler. Her focus was the habitual drunk driver, not the social drinker, and Lightner later worked for the alcohol industry. See, Lerner, *One for the Road*, 126.

43. Joyce M. Wolburg, "How Responsible Are 'Responsible' Drinking Campaigns for Preventing Alcohol Abuse?," *The Journal of Consumer Marketing* 22, no. 4 (2005): 176. For more on responsibility messages, see also, Katherine Clegg Smith, Samantha Cukier, and David H. Jernigan, "Defining Strategies for Promoting Product through 'Drink Responsibly' Messages in Magazine Ads for Beer, Spirits and Alcopops," *Drug Alcohol Dependence* 142 (2014): 168–73.

44. Smith, Cukier, and Jernigan, "Defining Strategies," 172.

45. I was unable to find an answer to why or how it was decided to omit reference to the drinking scene because the artist has a non-disclosure agreement with the film company.

Lesson Four: It's Funny When Kids Drink

1. Thank you to Hillary Chute for introducing me to and sharing this image. Elder can also be contextualized alongside other satirical cartoonists, most notably British artist Ronald Searle whose infamous drunken schoolgirls terrorize the campus of St. Trinian's school. For further analysis of Searle's work see, Elizabeth Marshall, *Graphic Girlhoods: Visualizing Education and Violence* (New York: Routledge, 2018), 95–99.

2. "*Saturday Evening Post* cover artists accounted for nearly 70 percent of the entire series," Jay R. Brooks, "In This Friendly, Freedom-Loving Land Of Ours—Beer Belongs . . . Enjoy It!—All About Beer," *All About Beer*, November 1, 2009, https://allaboutbeer.com/article/in-this-friendly-freedom-loving-land-of -ours%e2%80%94beer-belongs%e2%80%a6enjoy-it/. For more on this campaign, see Adam Houghtaling, "The Ads That Shaped American Beer Marketing," *PUNCH*, April 10, 2014, https://punchdrink.com/articles/the-ads-that-shaped-american-beer -marketing/. Beer manufacturers were also up against a political campaign from temperance advocates who sought to ban alcohol advertising. For a history of how beer manufacturers normalized drinking of the beverage via televised alcohol advertisements post WWII see, Pamela Pennock, "Televising Sin: Efforts to Restrict the Televised Advertisement of Cigarettes and Alcohol in the United States, 1950s to 1980s," *Historical Journal of Film, Radio and Television* 25, no. 4 (October 1, 2005): 619–36.

3. Nathan Abrams, "From Madness to Dysentery: *Mad's* Other New York Intellectuals," *Journal of American Studies* 37, no. 3 (2003): 439.

4. *MAD* was founded in 1952 as a comic book and then as a reaction to the establishment in 1954 of the Comics Code Authority became a magazine. For more on the history of *MAD* see, Maria Reidelbach, *Completely Mad: A History of the Comic Book and Magazine* (New York: Little Brown & Company, 1992); M. Thomas Inge, "Harvey Kurtzman and Modern American Satire," *Studies in American Humor*, no. 30 (2014): 25–40.

5. Harvey Kurtzman created Alfred E. Neuman from a postcard that he found in the early 1950s that featured the image and was captioned "Me Worry?" Neuman became the official cover boy for the publication beginning with the editorship of Al Feldstein in 1956. See also, Danny Lewis, "*MAD* Magazine's Iconic Alfred E. Neuman Turns 60 This Year," *Smithsonian*, March 17, 2016, https://www.smith sonianmag.com/smart-news/mad-magazines-iconic-alfred-e-neuman-turns-60-year -180958466/.

6. Abrams, "From Madness," 437.

7. Moritz Fink, "Culture Jamming in Prime Time: The Simpsons and the Tradition of Corporate Satire," in *Culture Jamming: Activism and the Art of Cultural Resistance*, eds. Marilyn DeLaure and Moritz Fink (New York: New York University Press, 2017), 256, dates the beginnings of corporate satire in America to 1885.

8. Yael M. Saiger, "Pulitzer Author Art Spiegelman Lectures on Comics and Judaism," *Harvard Crimson*, September 25, 2017, https://www.thecrimson.com/article /2017/9/25/art-spiegelman-comics/. Spiegelman worked for Topps from 1966 (then an 18-year-old summer intern) until 1989.

9. Topps Chewing Gum, Inc. also produced Bazooka bubble gum, and cartoonist Jay Lynch was the main writer for those comics from 1967 to 1990.

10. Sue Chastain, "Wacky Packs: The Hottest Thing Since Hula Hoops," 1974, https://clickamericana.com/toys-and-games/vintage-wacky-packages-candy-1970s

11. Jay Lynch, "How a Wacky Package Series Was Put Together," 2002, http:// www.wackypackages.org/history/production.html.

12. Art Spiegelman, "Wacky Days," in *Wacky Packages* (New York: Harry N. Abrams, Inc., 2008), 7–8.

13. Todd Leopold, "When Wacky Packages Ruled," *CNN*, August 12, 2008, http://edition.cnn.com/2008/SHOWBIZ/books/08/12/wacky.packages/index .html.

14. An example of this Alka Seltzer campaign can be viewed at https://www .youtube.com/watch?v=snZi5WA5gGE&ab_channel=3zy.

15. Alexander B. Joy, "How Polio Inspired the Creation of Candy Land," *The Atlantic*, July 28, 2019, https://www.theatlantic.com/technology/archive/2019/07/how -polio-inspired-the-creation-of-candy-land/594424/.

16. Cuteness as aesthetic has been theorized by Lori Merish, "Cuteness and Commodity Aesthetics: Tom Thumb and Shirley Temple," in *Freakery: Cultural Spectacles of the Extraordinary Body*, ed. Rosemarie Garland-Thomson (New York:

New York University Press, 1996), 185–203; Daniel Harris, *Cute, Quaint, Hungry and Romantic: The Aesthetics of Consumerism* (New York: Basic Books, 2000); and Sianne Ngai, "Our Aesthetic Categories," *PMLA* 125, no. 4 (September 11, 2010): 948–58.

17. Robin Bernstein, *Racial Innocence: Performing American Childhood From Slavery to Civil Rights* (New York: New York University Press, 2011), 34. For an analysis of the anti-cute and Black childhood, see Rebecca Wanzo, *The Content of Our Caricature: African American Comic Art and Political Belonging* (New York: New York University Press, 2020), 142.

18. Merish, "Cuteness and Commodity," 186.

19. Spiegelman, "Wacky Days," 8.

20. Vernard Eller, "The MAD Morality: An Exposé," *The Christian Century*, 1967, http://www.hccentral.com/eller1/cc122767.html.

21. See Spiegelman's introduction that discusses the controversial representation of childhood; an image of Boozin' Bruce can be found in The Topps Company, *Garbage Pail Kids* (New York: Abrams ComicArts, 2012), 20. Hillary Chute discusses Spiegelman and Garbage Pail Kids in, *Why Comics?: From Underground to Everywhere* (New York: HarperCollins Publishers, 2017).

22. Lynda Barry, *Picture This* (Montreal: Drawn & Quarterly, 2010), 15.

23. Hillary Chute, *Graphic Women: Life Narrative and Contemporary Comics* (New York: Columbia University Press, 2010), 112.

24. Lynda Barry, *Blabber, Blabber, Blabber* (Montreal: Drawn & Quarterly, 2011).

25. Mary Hambly, "An Interview with Lynda Barry," in *Backbone 4: Humor by Northwest Women* (Seattle: Seal Press, 1982), 26; 28. Much has been written about Barry's work. For more, see Chute, *Graphic Women*; Susan E. Kirtley, *Lynda Barry: Girlhood Through the Looking Glass* (Jackson: University Press of Mississippi, 2012).

26. Hillary Chute, "Still Tasting Perfect: An Appreciation of Lynda Barry by Hillary Chute," in *Drawn and Quarterly: Twenty-Five Years of Contemporary Cartooning, Comics, and Graphic Novels*, eds. Tom Devlin et al. (New York: Drawn & Quarterly, 2015), 569.

27. Rosemary Graham, "Dividing Them from Us Within Ourselves: A Conversation with Lynda Barry," *Iris: A Journal about Women*, no. 20 (Fall/Winter 1988): 36.

28. "Sneaking Out" was first published in 1990 in Art Spiegelman and Françoise Mouly's *RAW* 2, no. 2.

29. Lynda Barry, "Sneaking Out," in *Drawn and Quarterly: Twenty-Five Years of Contemporary Cartooning, Comics, and Graphic Novels*, eds. Tom Devlin et al. (New York: Drawn & Quarterly, 2015), 574.

30. Barry, "Sneaking Out," 576.

31. Ibid., 577.

32. Ibid.

33. Ibid.

34. Ibid., 578.

35. Ibid. See Lynda Barry, "What Pop Fly Gave His Daughter," in *Home Field: 9 Writers at Bat* (Seattle: Sasquatch Books, 1996), 71–82 for an autobiographical account of alcohol and fatherhood.

36. Pat Grant, "Lynda Barry on Comics, Creativity, and Matt Groening," *The Guardian*, November 02, 2016, https://www.theguardian.com/books/2016/nov/02/lynda-barry-on-comics-creativity-and-matt-groening-we-both-disdain-each-others-lives.

37. Lynda Barry, *It's So Magic* (New York: HarperPerennial, 1994), 125.

38. See Leigh Gilmore and Elizabeth Marshall, *Witnessing Girlhood: Toward a Tradition of Intersectional Life Writing* (New York: Fordham University Press, 2019) for an analysis of how comics artist Phoebe Gloeckner uses humor to upend familiar rape scripts.

39. Barry, *It's So Magic*, 58–59.

40. Ibid., 60.

41. Ibid., 61.

42. Ibid., 62.

43. Marshall, *Graphic Girlhoods*, 4.

44. Leigh Gilmore, *Tainted Witness: Why We Doubt What Women Say About Their Lives* (New York: Columbia University Press, 2017). See also, Leigh Gilmore, *The #MeToo Effect: What Happens When We Believe Women* (New York: Columbia University Press, 2023).

45. Barry, *It's So Magic*, 63.

46. Ibid., 67.

47. Ibid., 69.

48. Ibid.

49. Ibid.

50. Ibid., 71.

51. Bill Scher, "After Kavanaugh, #MeToo Should Launch a New Temperance Movement," *Politico*, October 09, 2018, https://www.politico.com/magazine/story/2018/10/09/kavanaugh-metoo-temperance-suffragettes-221141/. See also "Brock Turner's Statement Blames Sexual Assault on Stanford 'Party Culture,'" *The Guardian*, June 7, 2016, https://www.theguardian.com/us-news/2016/jun/07/brock-turner-statement-stanford-rape-case-campus-culture.

52. Lynda Barry, *Cruddy: An Illustrated Novel* (New York: Simon & Schuster, 1999).

Lesson Five: Mommy Needs a Cocktail

1. Charles Jewett, *The Youth's Temperance Lecturer* (Boston: Whipple and Damrell, 1841), 32.

2. Sarah W. Tracy, "Medicalizing Alcoholism One Hundred Years Ago," *Harvard Review of Psychiatry* 15, no. 2 (2007): 87. See also, Michelle L. McClellan, *Lady Lushes: Gender, Alcoholism, and Medicine in Modern America* (New Brunswick: Rutgers University Press, 2017).

3. Catherine Gilbert Murdock, *Domesticating Drink: Women, Men, and Alcohol in America, 1870–1940* (Baltimore: The Johns Hopkins University Press, 1998), 43.

4. Mallory O'Meara, *Girly Drinks: A World History of Women and Alcohol* (Ontario: Hanover Square Press, 2021), 153. See also, Madelon Powers, "Women and Public Drinking, 1890–1920," *History Today* 45, no. 2 (February 1, 1995): 46.

5. Murdock, *Domesticating Drink*, 45.

6. Ibid., 53.

7. Gabrielle Glaser, *Her Best-Kept Secret: Why Women Drink and How They Can Regain Control* (New York: Simon & Schuster, 2013), 70. Joe McKendry, "Sears, Roebuck Once Sold Bayer Heroin," *The Atlantic*, March 2019, https://www.theatlantic.com/magazine/archive/2019/03/sears-roebuck-bayer-heroin/580441/. For more on the history of motherhood and pharmaceuticals, see Jonathan M. Metzl, "'Mother's Little Helper': The Crisis of Psychoanalysis and the Miltown Resolution," *Gender & History* 15, no. 2 (2003): 228–55. See also, Murdock, *Domesticating Drink*, 50.

8. Viviana A. Zelizer, "The Price and Value of Children: The Case of Children's Insurance," *American Journal of Sociology* 86, no. 5 (1981): 72.

9. W. F. McNutt, "Mrs. Winslow's Soothing Syrup—A Poison," *American Journal of Pharmacy*, 1872, 221; "'Soothing Syrups,'" *The New York Times*, August 30, 1910, 6; "Soothing Syrup Kills Twins: Parents Gave Only Five Drops To Their Babies—Coroner Investigates," *The New York Times*, April 2, 1908, 1; "Soothing Syrups and Popular Remedies," *The New York Times*, 1885, 9.

10. "Motherhood," *Cosmopolitan*, May 1914, 154. For history of Pabst Malt Extract, see Anne Garner, "The 'Best' Tonic: Pabst Malt Extract Pamphlets in the Academy Library," *New York Academy of Medicine*, March 16, 2017, https://nyamcenterforhistory.org/2017/03/16/the-best-tonic-pabst-malt-extract-pamphlets-in-the-academy-library/#_ftnref3.

11. See Viviana A. Zelizer, *Pricing the Priceless Child: The Changing Social Value of Children* (New York: Basic Books, 1985); Daniel Thomas Cook, *The Commodification of Childhood: The Children's Clothing Industry and the Rise of the Child Consumer* (Durham, NC: Duke University Press, 2004).

12. Patrick Dillon, *The Much-Lamented Death of Madam Geneva: The Eighteenth-Century Gin Craze* (Boston: Justin, Charles & Co., 2003), 208.

13. Glaser, *Her Best-Kept*, 103.

14. Marian Sandmaier, *The Invisible Alcoholics: Women and Alcohol Abuse in America* (New York: McGraw-Hill Press, 1980).

15. Kevin Kenny and Helen Krull, *Sometimes My Mom Drinks Too Much* (Portsmouth: Heinemann, 1980), 17.

16. The Tonight Show Starring Jimmy Fallon, "Do Not Read: *Sometimes my Mom Drinks Too Much*, accessed May 24, 2023, https://www.google.com/search?q=jimmy+fallone+books+not+to+read+sometimes+my+mom+drinks+too+much&rlz=1C5CHFA_enCA1014CA1014&oq=jimmy+fallone+books+not+to+read+sometimes+my+mom+drinks+too+much&aqs=chrome..69i57.10674j0j9&sourceid=chrome&ie=UTF-8#fpstate=ive&vld=cid:cfd6df44,vid:nsxWnWFABGM.

17. Sandmaier, *The Invisible Alcoholics*, 57.

18. Lynda Barry, *Blabber, Blabber, Blabber* (Montreal: Drawn & Quarterly, 2011), 128.

19. Jan Waterson, *Women and Alcohol in Social Context: Mother's Ruin Revisited* (New York: Springer, 2000), 10.

20. Mark Jayne, Gill Valentine, and Sarah L. Holloway, *Alcohol, Drinking, Drunkenness: (Dis)Orderly Spaces* (Routledge, 2011), 126. See also, Lois A. West, "Negotiating Masculinities in American Drinking Subcultures," *The Journal of Men's Studies* 9, no. 3 (June 1, 2001): 371–92.

21. As Michelle Smirnova and Jennifer Gatewood Owens, "The New Mothers' Little Helpers: Medicalization, Victimization, and Criminalization of Motherhood via Prescription Drugs," *Deviant Behavior* 40, no. 8 (August 3, 2019): 960, note the 1980s is also the decade that saw the definition of *illicit* drugs such as crack and opiates as "antithetical to good mothering." This led to the criminalization of poor women, most of whom were also women of color, in the war on drugs. For more see, Sheigla Murphy and Paloma Sales, "Pregnant Drug Users: Scapegoats of Reagan/Bush and Clinton-Era Economics," *Social Justice* 28, no. 4 (February 14, 2001): 72–95.

22. Christie Mellor, *The Three-Martini Playdate: A Practical Guide to Happy Parenting* (San Francisco: Chronicle Books, 2004); Stefanie Wilder-Taylor, *Sippy Cups Are Not For Chardonnay* (New York: Simon Spotlight Entertainment, 2006); Stefanie Wilder-Taylor, *Nap Time Is the New Happy Hour: And Other Ways Toddlers Turn Your Life Upside Down* (New York: Simon Spotlight Entertainment, 2008).

23. Stacy Lu, "Cosmopolitan Moms: Adult Beverages Find Their Place at Children's Play Dates," *The New York Times*, November 9, 2006, G1.

24. Ashley Fetters, "Who Is a Wine Mom?," *The Atlantic*, May 23, 2020, https://www.theatlantic.com/family/archive/2020/05/wine-moms-explained/612001/.

25. "Mommy's Helper, in Red and White, and in the Courtroom, Too," *The New York Times*, April 23, 2011, https://www.nytimes.com/2011/04/24/weekinreview/24grist.html.

26. Julie Ma, "Q&A: Meet the 'Mommy' Behind MommyJuice Wines," *The Cut*, 2013, https://www.thecut.com/2013/04/qa-meet-the-mommy-behind-mommyjuice-wines.html.

27. Harmony Newman and Kyle Anne Nelson, "Mother Needs a Bigger 'Helper': A Critique of 'Wine Mom' Discourse as Conformity to Hegemonic Intensive Motherhood," *Sociology Compass* 15, no. 4 (2021): 1–10. See also Kelly D. Harding, Lisa Whittingham, and Kerry R. McGannon, "#sendwine: An Analysis of Motherhood, Alcohol Use and #winemom Culture on Instagram," *Substance Abuse: Research and Treatment* 15 (January 1, 2021): 1–9.

28. Newman and Nelson, "Mother Needs"; Joe Pinsker, "'Intensive' Parenting Is Now the Norm in America," *The Atlantic*, January 16, 2019, https://www.theatlantic.com/family/archive/2019/01/intensive-helicopter-parenting-inequality/580528/.

29. Kweilin Ellingrud and Liz Hilton Segel, "COVID-19 Has Driven Millions of Women out of the Workforce. Here's How to Help Them Come Back," *Fortune*,

February 13, 2021, https://fortune.com/2021/02/13/covid-19-women-workforce
-unemployment-gender-gap-recovery/.

30. Lisa Brown, *Baby, Mix Me a Drink* (San Francisco: McSweeney's, 2005).

31. "Reading Room," *O, The Oprah Magazine*, December 1, 2006.

32. Walter Benjamin, "Old Toys," in *Selected Writings Volume 2, 1927–1934,*
eds. Michael W. Jennings, Howard Eiland, and Gary Smith (Cambridge: Harvard
University Press, 1999), 101.

33. Lyranda Martin Evans and Fiona Stevenson, *Reasons Mommy Drinks* (New
York: Three Rivers Press, 2013); Mallory Langston, "The Dora the Explorer Cocktail,"
Salon, August 31, 2010, https://www.salon.com/2010/08/31/dora_the_explorer
_cocktail_open2010/.

34. Karen Valby, "'Moms, You've Entertained the Kids all day . . .': Hold up, Hold
Up. Why I'll Never be a NickMom," *Entertainment Weekly*, November 11, 2012,
https://ew.com/article/2012/11/11/nick-mom-never-going-to-happen/; Katie J.M. Baker,
"Welcome to Nickelodeon's New Channel for 'Bad Mommies,'" *Jezebel*, October 11,
2012, https://jezebel.com/welcome-to-nickelodeons-new-channel-for-bad-mommies
-5950358; John Jannarone, "Mom Shows Hurt Nick Jr.," *The Wall Street Journal*,
October 12, 2012, https://www.wsj.com/articles/SB1000087239639044374920457805 28
81834903510.

35. Baker, "Welcome to Nickelodeon's."

36. Marguerite Duras, *Practicalities* (New York: Grove Press, 1987), 17.

37. Sianne Ngai, "Our Aesthetic Categories," *PMLA* 125, no. 4 (September 11,
2010): 949.

38. Benjamin, "Old Toys," 100.

39. Anna Mae Duane, *Suffering Childhood in Early America: Violence, Race,
and the Making of the Child Victim* (Athens: University of Georgia Press, 2010), 11.

40. The battle between the cute and anti-cute child in popular culture is
elucidated by cultural theorist Daniel Harris, *Cute, Quaint, Hungry, and Romantic:
The Aesthetics of Consumerism* (New York: Basic Books, 2000), 19. See also, Gary
Cross, *The Cute and the Cool: Wondrous Innocence and Modern American
Children's Culture* (Oxford: Oxford University Press, 2004).

41. Linda Hutcheon, *A Theory of Parody: The Teachings of Twentieth-Century Art
Forms* (New York: Methuen, 1985), 75. For an insightful analysis of mothers
hedonistically partying across media, see Jo Littler, "Mothers Behaving Badly:
Chaotic Hedonism and the Crisis of Neoliberal Social Reproduction," *Cultural
Studies* 34, no. 4 (2020): 499–520.

Final Exam

1. Jessica Grose, "Mother's Little Helper Is Back, and Daddy's Partaking Too,"
The New York Times, October 3, 2020, https://www.nytimes.com/2020/10/03/style/am
-i-drinking-too-much.html; Gary Polakovic, "COVID-19 Drives Alcohol Sales, Raises
Concerns about Substance Abuse," *USCNews*, April 14, 2020, https://news.usc.edu
/168549/covid-19-alcohol-sales-abuse-stress-relapse-usc-experts/.

2. "Let Kids Drink," *Saturday Night Live*, May 19, 2020, https://www.youtube.com /watch?v=EGyTXmKpVlw&ab_channel=SaturdayNightLive.

3. See, for instance, Claire Cain Miller, "When Schools Closed, Americans Turned to Their Usual Backup Plan: Mothers," *The New York Times*, November 17, 2020, https://www.nytimes.com/2020/11/17/upshot/schools-closing-mothers-leaving -jobs.html. A 2020 article in *Fortune* pointed out that "80% of the 1.1 million people who exited the workforce were women, Kweilin Ellingrud and Liz Hilton Segel, "COVID-19 Has Driven Millions of Women out of the Workforce. Here's How to Help Them Come Back," *Fortune*, February 13, 2021, https://fortune.com/2021/02/13 /covid-19-women-workforce-unemployment-gender-gap-recovery/.

4. "SNL's Quarantine Sketch 'Let Kids Drink' Prompts Debate on Social Media," *Hollywood Reporter*, May 10, 2020, https://www.hollywoodreporter.com /news/general-news/snl-quarantine-sketch-let-kids-drink-prompts-debate-social -media-1294087/.

5. Michael Schneider, "The Simpsons Convinced Disney to Let Goofy and Homer Drink Beer Together," *Variety*, November 12, 2021, https://variety.com/2021/tv /news/the-simpsons-plusaversary-goofy-homer-beer-1235111097/?fbclid=IwAR3 -t72rRjstliTXeB3AJ5nZfkxb2hl-M-sZU2j4yKpJVFolxsN-2FohjgE. Thank you to Pete Kunze for this reference.

6. Michael Schneider, "The Simpsons."

7. Dr. Seuss, *The Cat in the Hat* (New York: Random House, 1957); Nick Perry and Paul Rosser, *Drink Me: Curious Cocktails from Wonderland* (Lexington: Rock Point, 2018).

8. Alex Williams, "The New Sobriety," *The New York Times*, 2019, https://www .nytimes.com/2019/06/15/style/sober-curious.html; Lily Rothman, "Inside the Shirley Temple: How Did the Mocktail Get Its Name?," *Time*, February 11, 2014, https://time .com/6659/shirley-temple-drink/.

9. Peter Pham, "These Baby Beer Bottles Will Let Tykes Kick Back Their Favorite Formula," *Foodbeast*, February 25, 2015, https://www.foodbeast.com/news/baby-beer/.

Index

Note: Illustrations are indicated by italicized page references

ELIZABETH MARSHALL is an associate professor at Simon Fraser University, where she teaches courses on children's literature, childhood, and popular culture. She is the author of *Graphic Girlhoods: Visualizing Education and Violence* (2018) and co-author with Leigh Gilmore of *Witnessing Girlhood: Toward an Intersectional Tradition of Life Writing* (2019).